Sainsbury's
magazine
cookbook

20 years of great cooking

Welcome

This year *Sainsbury's magazine* celebrated its 20th birthday and all of us who work on it are so proud of its great heritage, inspiring our millions of readers to cook delicious food for their families and friends. From the beginning, the magazine has provided brilliant triple-tested recipes from the best chefs and cookery writers – from the great Delia Smith, who launched the magazine in 1993 with her husband Michael Wynne-Jones, to Nigel Slater and other famous names such as Simon Hopkinson, Ruth Watson and Anna Del Conte. The present-day magazine continues this tradition, with new favourites such as Lorraine Pascale and Rachel Khoo. It also has its own highly skilled and talented cookery team who develop useful, delicious recipes month after month. This book is a celebration of the last 20 years, with many recipes from our leading writers and some that have become firm favourites – not only with us in the office, but also with the many readers who write and tell us how much they love them. I hope you enjoy using it as much as we enjoyed creating it!

Helena

Delia on the first issue of Sainsbury's magazine

contents

The Story Begins...

It's 1993, and Delia Smith and her journalist husband Michael Wynn-Jones launch a publication that promises to bring Sainsbury's and its customers closer together

On 28 April 1993 the first issue of *Sainsbury's magazine* hits the shelves, with Delia as its cover star. The only rule is that all ingredients featured must be available in at least 250 stores. Ruth Watson and Simon Hopkinson are part of the original team, as well as Nigel Slater, still one of the most popular contributors today. Italian writer Anna Del Conte and caterer to the stars, Lorna Wing will soon become regular faces, too.

April 1996

Chef Mark Hix (right) first appears in *Sainsbury's magazine* – 16 years later he will demonstrate how to cook the perfect steak and Yorkshire pud for our first-ever interactive issue.

2000

Lorna Wing's Sachertorte wedding cake appears – still the magazine's second most-requested recipe, it can be found on our blog.

June 2002

Sainsbury's magazine celebrates the Queen's Golden Jubilee with amazing party food ideas. Ten years later, Jubilee fever will strike again.

July 2003

The first food feature from Jamie Oliver (left) appears in the magazine and includes a recipe for a steak sarnie.

May 2007

Peggy Porschen, cake-maker to the stars, gives a decorating masterclass – we will see more of Peggy's handiwork on the cover of the October 2009 issue (left), which goes on to become a bestseller.

August 2007

Caribbean cook Levi Roots (right) explodes onto the scene with his Reggae Reggae sauce and is interviewed for the magazine's 'producers' feature. Some of his recipes will feature in the magazine in 2010.

June 2010

After cupcake mania, the trend for whoopie pies takes off – they even make it onto YouTube! *www.youtube.com/watch?v=zRa61w4mDJ4*

2011

Contributors include model-turned-baker, Lorraine Pascale, Richard Corrigan, Raymond Blanc, and Eric Lanlard. We also interview Ferran Adrià of El Bulli and LA favourite, Wolfgang Puck.

February 2012

TV's *The Great British Bake Off* reaches new heights of popularity. Winner Jo Wheatley's column will debut in the magazine a year later.

July 1993

An unlikely cover star is Michael Fish (right). This issue also showcases a couple of 'new' ingredients – including sun-dried tomatoes (sales of them instore increase by 90%) and rocket.

December 1993

Delia's recipe feature on cranberries also sees sales soar and is a taster for her successful *Winter Collection* book and 1995 TV series.

October 1994

Delia's trip to Japan prompts Sainsbury's to stock a range of Japanese foods. Also featured are recipes from Nigel Slater's *The 30-Minute Cook* – the book that will make him a household name.

July 1996

Alastair Hendy cooks Middle Eastern recipes. Yotam Ottolenghi and Sami Tamimi will later educate the nation more about Middle Eastern cuisine, leading Sainsbury's to sell a range of Middle Eastern ingredients, such as sumac and preserved lemons.

1998

Sainsbury's magazine's new contributors include Darina Allen of Ballymaloe Cookery School, Sybil Kapoor, and Rose and Ruth from The River Café.

April 1999

Nigella Lawson (left) writes her first column for the magazine. It will go on to become a quarterly series.

October 2003

Greg Wallace starts his column on British pub food – he won't be the last familiar face from *MasterChef* in the magazine.

2004

Antonio Carluccio (left), Gordon Ramsay, Bill Granger and Annie Bell all make their first appearances.

January 2006

Sam and Sam Clark create a Moorish New Year feast – their restaurant Moro is a firm favourite of the *Sainsbury's magazine* team.

September 2006

The 60-minute meals series debuts with Ching-He Huang. Roopa Gulati and James Martin will later follow.

November 2008

Thomasina Miers (right) wins *MasterChef* 2005, then goes on to open her own restaurant, Wahaca, in 2007. She shows readers how to cook Mexican food in this issue.

March 2010

A gluten-free polenta, lemon and pistachio cake is featured, a reflection of how the magazine has adapted to cater for all tastes and dietary requirements. Our most-requested recipe ever, it's on our blog.

September 2012

Sainsbury's magazine goes digital with the launch of its blog, *Kitchen Secrets* (sainsburysmagazine.co.uk), its first ever interactive cover complete with video content (October 2012), and a version of the magazine for tablets.

May 2013

Thank you to all our readers for your support over the last 20 years, we couldn't have done it without you...

Here's to the next 20!

Soups
and
Starters

Recipes

Hot chilli butternut squash soup

If you've never cooked butternut squash before, *Fiona Beckett*'s soup is a great way to start. Chilli perfectly complements its intense sweetness

Serves 6

Prep 15 mins **Total time** 1 hour 15 mins, plus cooling

Get ahead Make the soup, up to the end of step 4, a couple of days ahead, it freezes well too

- 1 butternut squash, weighing about 800g
- 3 tbsp sunflower or light olive oil
- good pinch saffron (about 20 threads)
- 570ml hot vegetable stock
- 1 medium-large onion, weighing about 175g, roughly chopped
- 1 garlic clove, crushed
- 1 rounded tsp each ground coriander, cumin and paprika
- 1 x 400g tin premium peeled plum tomatoes
- ½-1 tsp West Indian hot pepper sauce or chilli sauce (optional)

To serve
- 2 corn tortillas
- 250ml corn or sunflower oil
- 3 tbsp soured cream
- 2-3 tbsp roughly chopped fresh coriander leaves
- a few chilli flakes (optional)

1 Preheat the oven to 190°C, fan 170°C, gas 5. Wipe the butternut squash with a damp cloth, cut it in half lengthways and scoop out the seeds. Put 1 tablespoon of the oil in a roasting tin and turn the squash in the oil, laying the 2 halves, cut-side down, in the tin. Bake for about 40 minutes, or until soft, leave to cool for 15 minutes.

2 Meanwhile, soak the saffron threads in 2 tablespoons of the hot stock.

3 Gently fry the onion in the remaining 2 tablespoons of oil for 10 minutes, until soft but not coloured. Add the crushed garlic, coriander, cumin and paprika, and fry for another minute. Then add the plum tomatoes and their juices. Crush the tomatoes with a wooden spoon and cook for about 5 minutes, until you have a pulpy sauce.

4 Scoop the pulp out of the squash and place in a blender or food processor, along with any juices from the roasting tin, the saffron-infused stock and the pulpy tomato and onion sauce, and blitz until completely smooth. (You may have to do this in 2 batches.) Pour the soup into a large saucepan and stir in the remaining stock. Add the West Indian hot pepper sauce or chilli sauce, if using, and salt to taste.

5 Cut the tortillas into fine strips. Heat the oil in a wok over a medium heat until the oil is nearly smoking (about 4 minutes) and drop in the tortilla strips, a few at a time. They should turn golden and crisp in about 30 seconds. Remove with a slotted spoon and drain on kitchen towel.

6 To serve, ladle the soup into 6 warmed bowls, drizzle with soured cream, scatter over chopped coriander leaves and top with the crispy tortilla strips. And chilli addicts, sprinkle with chilli flakes!

■ 248cals; 14.5g fat (2.2g sat fat); 4.6g protein; 4.4g fibre; 24.8g carbs; 9g total sugars; 0.24g salt

KITCHEN *Secret*

Roasting the squash produces a wonderfully soft pulp that gives soup a super-smooth, velvety texture.

Beetroot soup with crème fraîche

Beetroot has a gorgeous, earthy flavour and beautiful colour.
It makes a change from the usual root vegetables for soup

Serves 4
Prep 5 mins **Total time** 1 hr 10 mins
Get ahead Make up to 2 days ahead.
Can also be frozen

- **2 x 500g bunches beetroot,
  peeled and cut into wedges**
- **3 tbsp olive oil**
- **2 tbsp thyme leaves**
- **75g butter**
- **1.5 litres hot vegetable stock**
- **4 tbsp crème fraîche**

1 Preheat the oven to 220°C, fan 200°C,
gas 7. Put the beetroot in a roasting
tin and drizzle with the olive oil.
Scatter over half the thyme leaves
and season. Roast, covered with foil,
for 45 minutes until tender.
2 Shred one or two wedges of roasted
beetroot and set aside. Put the butter
in a pan and melt over a low heat. Add
the remaining roasted beetroot, along
with any juices, and most of the
remaining thyme leaves. Fry gently for
a minute or two, then add the stock
and bring to the boil. Simmer, partially
covered, for 20 minutes. Purée and
season the soup, then serve garnished
with crème fraîche, shredded beetroot
and thyme leaves.

■ 393cals; 32.2g fat (15.7g sat fat);
7.3g protein; 6.3g fibre; 18.1g carbs;
17.1g total sugars; 0.73g salt

ON THE SIDE
Feta, spring onion
and garlic toasts

Roast **garlic cloves** at 180°C, fan 160°C,
gas 4 for 10-15 minutes until soft. Toast
slices of **baguette** and top with **feta**,
sliced **spring onion** and the roasted garlic.

■ 206cals; 6.1g fat (3.6g sat fat);
9.4g protein; 2.3g fibre; 28.3g carbs;
1.9g total sugars; 1.7g salt

KITCHEN
Secret

To save time, use
ready-cooked beetroot
(vacuum-packed, not
beetroot in vinegar) and
start at step 2.

'A LOVELY, UNUSUAL SOUP THAT *looks as good* AS IT TASTES'

Rich chicken and garlic broth with winter vegetables

This meal-in-a-bowl is from *Alex Mackay* who has worked for Raymond Blanc and is a popular cookery teacher and writer

Serves 4
Prep 40 min **Total time** 3 hrs 30 mins
Get ahead Make the stock and the mayonnaise, slice the cooked chicken and chop the chilli and chives up to 2 days ahead. Store covered, separately, in the fridge

For the stock
  1 x 1.8kg chicken
  3 tbsp soy sauce
  2 large onions, peeled and halved
  8 garlic cloves, peeled and halved
  ½ x 15g pack fresh thyme
  3 bay leaves
  12 peppercorns
For the broth
  1.5 litres chicken stock (above)
  6 Chantenay carrots, peeled and halved lengthways, or 2 large carrots, peeled and thickly sliced
  2 small turnips, peeled and cut in 6 wedges
  2 small leeks, thickly sliced
  the breasts from the cooked chicken (see above)
  1 x 25g pack fresh chives, finely chopped
  1 small red chilli, deseeded and finely chopped
  cayenne pepper, to taste
For the mayonnaise
  1 large egg yolk
  2 tsp Dijon mustard

  1 garlic clove, crushed
  100ml vegetable oil
  100ml extra-virgin olive oil

1 Place the chicken in a large saucepan. Cover with cold water and stir in the soy sauce. Bring to the boil and skim off as much of the initial scum as you can, using a ladle.

2 Add the onions and garlic, the thyme and bay leaves (tied in a bundle), and the peppercorns. Simmer gently for 2 hours, then lift out the chicken and set aside. Don't worry about skimming as the stock simmers – the fat on top enriches the broth.

3 Strain the stock through a colander or large sieve into a bowl. Discard the vegetables and herbs. (You will have more stock than you need for this recipe but, once cooled, it will keep for a week in a plastic container in the fridge. It also freezes well.)

4 Bring 1.5 litres of the stock to the boil, reduce the heat and add the carrots and turnips. Simmer for 15 minutes, add the leeks and simmer for 10 minutes. Carve the breasts off the chicken, remove the skin, and slice each breast into 6. Add to the stock and warm through for 5 minutes.

5 While the vegetables are cooking, make the mayonnaise. In a large bowl, whisk together the egg yolk, half a teaspoon of salt, the mustard and crushed garlic. Add the vegetable oil, drip by drip, whisking until emulsified. Add 1 tablespoon of hot water followed by the olive oil in a slow steady stream.

6 Ladle a quarter of the hot broth into the mayonnaise and whisk in quickly. Pour this mixture back into the pan and stir over a low heat for 2 minutes – do not boil or it may curdle. Add the chopped chives and chilli. Season with salt and cayenne pepper, and serve. **Note:** this recipe contains raw/ partially cooked eggs.

■ 595cals; 41.6g fat (6.1g sat fat); 25.6g protein; 6.3g fibre; 9g carbs; 8.4g total sugars; 1.4g salt

Also try shredding leftover chicken into some of the remaining stock with noodles, chilli, ginger and soy sauce.

Parsley soup with caper and tomato salsa

Parsley is a main ingredient, rather than just a garnish, in this soup by *Sarah Randell*. To save time, you could buy ready-made croutons

Serves 4
Prep 15 mins **Total time** 45 mins
Get ahead Make up to 2 days
in advance. Can also be frozen

- a knob of butter
- 2 shallots, chopped
- 300g potato, chopped
- 750ml hot vegetable
- or chicken stock
- 200ml milk
- whole nutmeg, for grating
- 1 tbsp Dijon mustard
- 150g curly-leaf parsley, tough
- stalks removed, chopped
- 16 SunBlush tomatoes, chopped
- 1 tbsp small capers

For the croutons
- 8 slices of French bread
- olive oil for drizzling

1 Heat the butter in a large pan, add the shallots and potato and cook over a medium heat for 10 minutes. Add the stock, bring to the boil and simmer until the potato is tender, about 15 minutes.
2 Add the milk, a generous grating of nutmeg, the mustard and chopped parsley, and bring the mixture to simmering point. Immediately take the pan off the heat and leave to cool slightly. Liquidise the soup in a blender, in batches, until smooth.
3 For the croutons, preheat the oven to 200°C, fan 180°C, gas 6. Drizzle the bread slices with olive oil and bake for 3-4 minutes until golden, turning them halfway.
4 Return the soup to the pan, season to taste and gently reheat. Pour into serving bowls and top the soup with the croutons, chopped SunBlush tomatoes and the capers.
- 336cals; 13g fat (4g sat fat); 8g protein; 39g carbs; 8g total sugars; 2.1g salt

KITCHEN
Secret

For easy chopping, wash the parsley first and pat dry with kitchen paper – you'll find it easier to chop when damp.

Chickpea and chorizo soup

This recipe is by **_Tamsin Burnett-Hall_**, who worked at the magazine with Delia in the early days. It's a winter warmer with a hit of spicy flavour

Serves 4
Prep 15 mins **Total time** 30 mins
Get ahead Make the soup a couple of days ahead. Can also be frozen

- **1 large onion, chopped**
- **2 tbsp olive oil**
- **2 garlic cloves**
- **4 tsp chopped rosemary**
- **3 x 410g tins chickpeas, drained and rinsed**
- **850ml chicken stock**
- **100g chorizo, skinned and diced**

1. In a large saucepan, soften the onion in the olive oil over a medium heat for 8-10 minutes until golden. Crush the garlic and stir into the onion with half the rosemary, then cook for a further 2 minutes.
2. Add two-thirds of the chickpeas, all of the stock and plenty of seasoning to the pan. Bring to the boil, cover and simmer briskly for 5 minutes.
3. Meanwhile, dry-fry the diced chorizo in a small frying pan for 2 minutes over a medium heat, until the chorizo is crisp and has released its oil. Stir in the remaining rosemary and sizzle for about 15 seconds before removing from the heat.
4. Blend the soup until smooth, then stir in the rest of the chickpeas. Check the seasoning and warm through for 1-2 minutes.
5. Ladle the soup into warm bowls, and spoon over the chorizo and its oil. Serve with toasts, or croutons too, if you want to make the soup more substantial, see pages 12 and 16.
- 398cals; 16.8g fat (3.7g sat fat); 18.4g protein; 10.9g fibre; 31.6g carbs; 3.4g total sugars; 2g salt

KITCHEN
Secret

Tinned chickpeas make the soup fuss-free. Try adding them to salads and stews, too.

Raymond Blanc

Raymond's Roquefort soufflés are an impressive French classic that can be prepared in advance and are ideal for easy entertaining

Passionate Frenchman Raymond Blanc is chef patron at the world renowned Le Manoir aux Quat'Saisons and also owns a string of Brasserie Blanc restaurants across the country. He was awarded an honorary OBE in 2007 and holds two Michelin stars for his Oxfordshire restaurant at Le Manoir, definitely one to add to your little black book.

'SERVE THE SOUFFLES WITH AN *apple, celery and walnut* SALAD'

Roquefort cheese soufflés

Serves 4
Prep 20 mins **Total time** 40 mins
Get ahead Make to the end of step
5 the day before, chill; reheat for
10 minutes to serve

To line the dishes
  25g soft unsalted butter
  25g dry fine breadcrumbs, plus
  extra for coating
For the base
  25g unsalted butter
  25g plain flour
  150ml whole milk
  75g Roquefort cheese, crumbled
For the soufflé mix
  a squeeze of lemon juice
  5 medium egg whites
  sea salt

1 Brush the insides of 4 x 200ml
   ramekins with the butter using a
   pastry brush. Sprinkle over the
   breadcrumbs so they coat the dishes
   completely, tipping out any excess.

2 Preheat the oven to 200°C, fan 180°C,
   gas 6 and place a baking tray on the
   middle shelf of the oven to preheat.
   Put the butter and flour in a pan over
   a medium heat and stir for 4-5
   minutes without letting it colour.
   Gradually stir in the milk to form a
   béchamel sauce. Lower the heat and
   continue to cook for 5 minutes, stirring
   now and then. Remove from the heat
   and leave to cool a little, then add the
   cheese and stir until melted into the
   mix. Transfer to a large bowl.

3 In a separate bowl, whisk the lemon
   juice with the egg whites until very
   soft peaks form. Add two pinches of
   sea salt and continue whisking until
   you have soft (not firm) peaks. Quickly
   whisk a third of the egg whites into
   the cheese mixture to lighten the base,
   then carefully fold in the remaining
   egg whites. Check the seasoning,
   adding sea salt and freshly ground
   black pepper, if necessary.

4 Fill the soufflé dishes to the top
   with the mixture. Hold a spatula flat
   against the rim of the dishes and
   scrape any excess mixture away from
   the top. Run your thumb and index
   finger around the rim of the dishes
   – this will loosen the soufflé mixture
   from the edge so it can rise more
   easily and evenly. Put the dishes on
   the preheated baking tray and bake
   for 15 minutes. Remove from the
   oven and leave to cool.

5 Loosen the soufflés from their dishes
   and invert them on to a tray lightly
   coated with breadcrumbs. Turn them
   in the crumbs until lightly coated.

6 Preheat the oven again to 200°C,
   fan 180°C, gas 6. Reheat the soufflés
   in shallow ovenproof dishes or on
   a baking tray for about 5 minutes
   until piping hot.

■ 251cals; 18g fat (12g sat fat);
  10g protein; 1g fibre; 12g carbs;
  2g total sugars; 1.1g salt

'SIMPLE, WITH *delicate flavours*
AND REAL WOW FACTOR, TOO'

Seared scallops with minted peas and broad beans

If you're looking for something to serve for a special occasion, this elegant starter by *Gordon Ramsay* is just the ticket

Serves 4

Prep 30 mins **Total time** 45 mins
Get ahead You can blanch the peas, and blanch and pod the broad beans several hours ahead

315g podded broad beans, thawed if frozen
250g podded peas, thawed if frozen
1 small bunch fresh thyme, leaves only
1 tsp coarse sea salt
24 large scallops, roes removed
1-2 tbsp olive oil
a small knob of butter
a generous handful of fresh mint, leaves chopped
extra-virgin olive oil, to drizzle

1 Bring a pan of salted water to the boil, tip in the broad beans and blanch for 3-4 minutes or until tender. Drain well, refresh in iced water and drain again. Gently squeeze the broad beans to pop them out of their skins. Meanwhile, return the water to the boil and blanch the peas for 3-4 minutes or until tender. Drain and refresh in iced water, then tip into a bowl with the broad beans and set aside.

2 Put the thyme leaves on a chopping board and sprinkle with 1 teaspoon of coarse sea salt. Chop finely, then sprinkle the thyme salt over one side of the scallops. Heat a large griddle or frying pan (or 2 frying pans) and add 1 tablespoon of olive oil.

3 Pan-fry the scallops for 1½ minutes on each side, depending on their thickness – when cooked, they should feel slightly springy to the touch. Add a little more oil, if necessary. Remove to a warm plate and rest for a minute while you reheat the vegetables.

4 Tip the peas and broad beans into the frying pan and add a splash of water and the small knob of butter. Heat for a minute to warm through, season to taste and stir in the chopped mint.

5 Spoon the vegetables on to warm plates and top with the scallops. Drizzle a little extra-virgin olive oil around each plate and serve.

■ 248cals; 7.8g fat (1.8g sat fat); 29.7g protein; 7.7g fibre; 15.9g carbs; 2.5g total sugars; 0.7g salt

KITCHEN *Secret*

To ensure even cooking, turn the scallops halfway through cooking in the same order as you put them into the pan.

HEALTHY APPETITE BY GORDON RAMSAY (QUADRILLE, £14.99)

Chicken, pancetta and prune terrine

This terrine by **Brian Glover** makes a very special starter. Serve it with chutney, pickles and crusty white bread

Serves 8-10

Prep 30 mins **Total time** 2 hrs, plus 2 hrs' marinating and overnight chilling **Get ahead** Make up to the end of step 4 a few days ahead; the terrine can be frozen at this stage, too

- **4 medium skinless chicken breasts**
- **1 garlic clove, finely chopped**
- **3 tsp chopped tarragon**
- **1 tsp chopped thyme**
- **1 tbsp olive oil**
- **150ml white vermouth or white port**
- **20 ready-to-eat pitted prunes**
- **200g young-leaf spinach**
- **1 x 28g pack fresh flat-leaf parsley, chopped**
- **100g cubetti di pancetta**
- **2 x 105g packs smoked pancetta slices**

1 Cut the chicken into long strips about 1cm thick. Put them in a non-metallic dish with the garlic, 1 teaspoon of the tarragon, the thyme, olive oil and vermouth or port. Season, tuck in the prunes, cover and marinate in the fridge for at least 2 hours (up to 8 hours).

2 Preheat the oven to 180°C, fan 160°C, gas 4. Put the spinach in a colander, pour over a kettleful of boiling water, drain, refresh under cold water, then drain again. Squeeze out the excess water with your hands, then mix with the parsley and remaining tarragon. Remove the prunes from the marinade and set aside. Tip the chicken into a

sieve over a bowl to drain, then stir the cubetti di pancetta into the chicken.

3 Prepare a 900g loaf tin (or terrine measuring 23 x 12cm x 7.5cm deep) by lining it with clingfilm, so the clingfilm hangs over the edges of the tin. Then, line the tin with overlapping pancetta slices, letting them hang over the edge, too. Layer on the chicken, the prunes and the spinach mixture, beginning and ending with chicken, seasoning each layer. When the tin is full, spoon over the reserved marinade. Fold over the loose ends of the pancetta and top with any remaining slices. Cover the tin tightly with foil.

4 Place the tin in a larger roasting tin and pour in boiling water to come just over halfway up the sides of the loaf tin. Place in the oven and cook for 1 hour 15 minutes-1 hour 30 minutes, testing after the shorter time. The terrine should have shrunk from the sides of the tin and the chicken be tender to a sharp knife. Cool, covered. Once cold, stand the tin on a plate, replace the top foil with clean foil and put weights, 2 tins or a bag of sugar, on top. Chill overnight in the fridge.

5 To finish, tip off any excess liquid from the top of the terrine, turn out on to a plate and strip off the clingfilm. Cut into slices using a very sharp knife.

■ 312cals; 16.3g fat (5.1g sat fat); 26.6g protein; 2.3g fibre; 10.9g carbs; 9g total sugars; 1.5g salt

KITCHEN *Secret*

Pancetta is smoked and has a smoky-sweet flavour, but rashers of streaky bacon also work well in this recipe.

Thomasina Miers

This is a great 'dig in and share' starter for the summer months. If the sun shines, barbecue the prawns

Since winning the BBC's *MasterChef* in 2005, Thomasina Miers has written three cookery books, co-presented two TV series and opened several hugely successful Wahaca Mexican restaurants in London. For anyone who wants to learn about Mexican food, her book *Mexican Food Made Simple* is a must-have.

Chilli prawns

Serves 8

Prep 15 mins **Total time** 1 hr 30 mins, plus (optional) marinating
Get ahead Make the marinade up to a week ahead; chill in a sealed container

- 40 raw tiger or king prawns
- 8 warm tortillas
- lime wedges and a handful of coriander, to serve

For the marinade
- 25g dried chipotle chillies or
- ½ x 11g pack whole dried chillies
- 1 large onion, roughly chopped
- ¾ head of garlic, broken up into cloves and peeled
- 2 small bay leaves (ideally fresh)
- ½ tbsp oregano leaves or a pinch of dried oregano
- ½ tbsp thyme leaves
- ¼ tsp cumin seeds, crushed
- 2 dried ancho chillies (optional)
- 75ml olive oil
- 45ml white wine vinegar
- ½ tbsp balsamic vinegar
- ½ tbsp tomato purée
- 1 tbsp demerara or palm sugar
- sea salt

1 First, make the marinade. Wash the dried chillies in cold water and drain. Snip off the stalk end of each chilli, then cover the chillies with cold water in a medium pan and simmer for 30-40 minutes until completely soft. Rinse off any excess seeds.

2 Put the onion, garlic, herbs and cumin in a blender with 50ml water, the ancho chillies, if using, and 2 of the softened chillies. Purée to a smooth paste.

3 Heat the olive oil in a small heavy-based pan. Add the chilli paste and fry for 3 minutes, stirring continuously with a spatula. Add the vinegars, tomato purée, sugar, ½ tablespoon of sea salt and 25ml water, and cook for 5 minutes before adding the rest of the softened chillies. Cook, stirring, for another 15 minutes, then check if it needs more salt or sugar. Leave to cool before blending to a rough paste. Toss the prawns in the chilli marinade (reserving a few tablespoons). Leave to marinate for an hour or two if you have time.

4 When you're ready to eat, griddle, fry or barbecue the prawns for a few minutes each side until pink, then smear with a dab of the reserved chilli. Serve with warm tortillas, lime wedges and some coriander.

■ 274cals; 8g fat (1g sat fat); 15g protein; 1.7g fibre; 37g carbs; 2g total sugars; 0.8g salt

Thai-style gravadlax with coriander and lime dressing

Ruth Watson started writing for the magazine from the first issue in May 1993. This is a great starter for a crowd

Serves 8-10

Prep 30 mins **Total time** 30 mins, plus 2 days' marinating

Get ahead You can marinate the salmon up to 5 days before serving. The sauce will keep, covered, in the fridge for up to 3 days

2 skin-on sides of salmon

For the pickling mixture

3 level tbsp sea salt

3 level tbsp white sugar

5cm-piece of root ginger, peeled and grated

3 sticks of lemon grass, sliced very finely

grated zest of 3 lemons

1 level tsp Thai 7-spice seasoning (optional)

2 tsp black peppercorns, coarsely crushed

1 medium red chilli, deseeded and finely chopped

3 tbsp chopped fresh coriander leaves

For the coriander and lime dressing

2 medium egg yolks

2 level tsp Dijon mustard

2 level tsp caster sugar

225ml groundnut oil

2.5cm piece of root ginger, peeled and grated

juice of 1 large lime

2 tbsp chopped coriander

4 tbsp crème fraîche

1 Combine all the pickling ingredients in a bowl. Divide the mixture into 2 quarters and 1 half. In a long, shallow dish, or tray just big enough for the salmon, spread a quarter of the mixture in an approximation of the fish shape. Place one of the sides, skin-side down, on the mixture.

2 Spread the half portion of mixture over the flesh, covering it evenly, and then place the second side of the salmon on top to make a 'whole' fish. Rub the remaining quarter of pickling mixture into the skin.

3 Cover the fish with a piece of foil and then weight it down, first with a board or lid and then with some heavy tins or weights. Put the dish in the refrigerator and leave it to marinate in the pickle for a minimum of 2 days, turning the fish each day.

4 To make the dressing, whisk the egg yolks, mustard and sugar together vigorously. Then, very slowly at first, add the groundnut oil until you have a fairly thick dressing. Now whisk in the ginger, lime juice and coriander, then season to taste. Leave for 6 hours for the flavours to develop, then just before serving it with the gravadlax, whisk in the crème fraîche. **Note:** this recipe contains raw/ partially cooked eggs

■ 468cals; 39g fat (9g sat fat); 22g protein; 0g fibre; 2.9g carbs; 2.9g total sugars; 1.2g salt

KITCHEN *Secret*

Want a smaller quantity? Buy a good-size tail piece of salmon and halve the pickling ingredients.

'MAKE PLENTY – THEY'LL BE *snapped up* BY YOUR GUESTS. SERVE THEM WITH *something sparkly* TO GET THE PARTY STARTED'

Celebration canapés

Planning a party? Pick and choose from our selection of simple but impressive nibbles and get some bottles chilling in the fridge

Florentine pizzettes

Stamp out 12 x 9cm rounds from 2 ready-made **pizza bases**. Spread with **sundried tomato bruschetta topping**. Wilt 200g **young-leaf spinach** in a pan, then drain and season. Divide between the pizzettes and make a dip in the centre of each one. Break a **quail's egg** into each dip and top with torn **mozzarella**. Bake for 7 minutes at 200°C, fan 180°C, gas 6. Sprinkle with grated **parmesan** and bake for a further 6-8 minutes. **Makes 12**.

- 190cals; 6.2g fat, (3.3g sat fat); 8.8g protein; 1.7g fibre; 26.4g carbs; 4.5g total sugars; 0.6g salt

Coconut prawn fritters

Sift 75g **self-raising flour** into a bowl. Whisk in 1 **large egg yolk** with 75ml **coconut milk** and season. Beat the egg white until it forms peaks, then fold into the batter with 18 chopped **raw peeled tiger prawns**. Heat a little **vegetable oil** in a large frying pan and cook tablespoons of the mixture for 1-2 minutes, then flip and cook on the other side. Serve hot with **sweet chilli sauce. Makes 15**.

- 52cals; 2.8g fat (1g sat fat); 2.9g protein; 0.2g fibre; 3.7g carbs; 0.1g total sugars; 0.2g salt

Smoked salmon bruschetta

Thinly slice a half ciabatta into rounds, then griddle until golden on both sides. Top with **créme fraîche**, **smoked salmon**, peeled and finely sliced **red onion**, a few **capers** and **rocket**. **Makes 12**.

- 117cals; 8.2g fat (4.6g sat fat); 4.9g protein; 0.4g fibre; 5.9g carbs; 0.7g total sugars, 0.8g salt

Chilli coriander sausage rolls

Squeeze the meat from 4 **chilli and coriander pork sausages** (or other sausages) into a bowl. Mix with 1 tablespoon of chopped **fresh coriander** and the zest of 1 **lime**. Unroll 1 x 375g pack **fresh ready-rolled puff pastry** and cut in half lengthways. Put the sausagemeat down the centre of each length, brush the edges with **beaten egg**, then fold over and press to seal. Brush with more egg and sprinkle with **sesame seeds**. Cut each piece into 8 sausage rolls. Bake on a baking sheet at 200°C, fan 180°C, gas 6 for 20 minutes. **Makes 16**.

- 119cals; 8.4g fat (4.5g sat fat); 2.7g protein; 0.2g fibre; 9.3g carbs; 0.5g total sugars; 0.3g salt

AND TO DRINK...
Clementine Prosecco cocktail

In a pan, mix together the juice of 6 **clementines** and ½ **lemon** with 100g **caster sugar**. Slowly bring to a simmer, stirring all the time until the sugar has dissolved. Increase the heat and bubble the mixture for 5 minutes until syrupy. Leave to cool, then chill. To serve, pour a little chilled clementine syrup into 6 Champagne flutes, followed by a dash of **Campari or Aperol**. Top up with a bottle of chilled **Prosecco** and stir. **Serves 6**.

KITCHEN Secret

Don't wait for a celebration – choose one of the canapés and make a batch for a supper party starter.

Salads and Light Lunches

Recipes

Devilled Caesar salad with Parma ham

This lower-fat Caesar salad by *Gordon Ramsay* includes crispy fried Parma ham – it's every bit as delicious as the well-known classic

Serves 4
Prep time 20 mins
Total time 40 mins, plus cooling
Get ahead Make the dressing a day ahead and keep chilled

6-8 slices Parma ham
olive oil
8 thick slices ciabatta
4 Little Gem lettuces, trimmed
15-16 marinated anchovy fillets
extra-virgin olive oil, to drizzle
parmesan shavings, to finish
For the dressing
1 garlic clove, crushed
2 anchovies in olive oil (from a tin) rinsed, drained and finely chopped
½ tsp paprika
a splash of Worcestershire sauce
100g natural or Greek yogurt

1 For the dressing, whiz together all the ingredients in a small food processor or blender and season with freshly ground pepper to taste. The anchovies will probably provide enough salt.

2 Next, crisp the Parma ham in two batches. Heat a tiny drizzle of olive oil in a large nonstick frying pan and lay half of the ham slices in the pan. Fry over a low-medium heat for a few minutes on each side until golden brown, then transfer to a plate. Cook the rest of the ham in the same way. Leave to cool.

3 Meanwhile, lightly toast the ciabatta slices in the same pan, turning the bread to colour it on both sides. Remove and cut into chunky croutons.

4 Break the Parma ham slices into smaller pieces. Separate the lettuce leaves and divide between serving plates with the croutons, Parma ham and anchovies. Drizzle over the dressing and a little olive oil and scatter over parmesan to serve.

■ 400cals; 12.8g fat, (5.1g sat fat); 28.4g protein; 2.2g fibre; 47.5g carbs; 6g total sugars; 4.6g salt

KITCHEN Secret

Add griddled chicken or quartered hardboiled eggs if you want to make this salad more substantial.

HEALTHY APPETITE BY GORDON RAMSAY (QUADRILLE, £14.99)

Ching-He Huang

Ching first had fried chilli squid in London at the Royal China restaurant – this is her easy version. Serve with sweet chilli sauce. Yum!

Taiwanese-born British food writer Ching-He Huang is a familiar face on our television screens. Ching's accessible cooking style and recipe writing has made Chinese cookery achievable for many of our readers and her best-selling cookbooks are testament to her success.

Fried chilli squid salad

Serves 2 generously
Prep 15 mins **Total time** 30 mins

**250g prepared squid, tentacles
separated and tubes sliced
into rings**
1 large egg, beaten
6 tbsp cornflour
1 tsp crushed dried chillies
½ tsp freshly ground black pepper
275ml vegetable oil, for frying
¼ iceberg lettuce, shredded
**1 carrot, trimmed, peeled
and thinly sliced into strips**
**1 large spring onion, trimmed
and sliced lengthways**
**1 red chilli, deseeded and
thinly sliced**
2-3 tbsp coriander leaves
sweet chilli sauce, to serve

1 Dip the squid rings into the beaten
egg. Season the cornflour with
the crushed chillies, pepper and
½ teaspoon of sea salt, then dust
the squid generously with the flour.

2 Heat the oil in a wok or large saucepan
over a high heat to 180°C or until a
cube of bread dropped in turns
golden brown in 15 seconds. Fry
the squid in batches until golden,
removing it with a slotted spoon
as it is ready.

3 Serve the squid on a bed of
shredded lettuce and carrot strips
and sprinkle with the spring onion,
chilli and coriander leaves. Serve
with sweet chilli sauce.

■ 407cals; 17.4g fat, (2.9g sat fat);
24.4g protein; 2g fibre; 38.2g carbs;
4.6g total sugars; 0.56g salt

Roasted vegetable salad with Camembert dressing

The Camembert in this recipe by *Alex Mackay* makes a luxurious coating for the vegetables, which can be varied to suit the season

Serves 4
Prep time 30 mins
Total time 1 hr 30 mins
Get ahead Make the croutons up to 2 days in advance, store in an airtight container

- 1 half-baguette, sliced into 20 pieces on an angle
- 60g soft unsalted butter
- 4 medium beetroot
- 4 small parsnips
- 10 Chantenay carrots
- 2 heads of chicory
- 5 tbsp groundnut or vegetable oil
- 3 tbsp red wine vinegar
- 60g hazelnuts
- 3 small pears
- two handfuls of watercress

For the dressing
- 1 x 250g Camembert, chilled
- 3 tbsp crème fraîche

1 Preheat the oven to 200°C, fan 180°C, gas 6. For the croutons, lightly spread each slice of baguette with butter. Arrange in a single layer on a baking sheet and bake in the preheated oven for 5 minutes or until golden. Set aside.

2 To cook the vegetables, peel and quarter the beetroot. Peel the parsnips and halve them and the carrots lengthways. Cut each head of chicory in half lengthways, too. Spread a large piece of tin foil on a small baking tray. Place the beetroots on half the tin foil. Spoon over 2 tbsp of the oil and 1 tbsp of vinegar. Sprinkle over the hazelnuts and season. Fold the other half of the foil over the top, seal the edges tightly and bake for 50 minutes in the preheated oven.

3 Meanwhile bring a large pot of salted water to the boil, add the carrots and parsnips and boil for 4 minutes, add the chicory and boil for a further 3 minutes. Drain the vegetables, then pat dry with kitchen paper.

4 Place the parsnips, cut-side down, on a large roasting tray, along with the carrots and halved chicory, all in a single layer. Finally, cut 2 of the pears into quarters, removing the pips, and add those, too. Spoon over the remaining oil and vinegar, and season well.

5 Roast the vegetables and pears on the top shelf of the oven, above the beetroot, for 30 minutes, then remove the tray from the oven and dot the vegetables and pears with the remaining butter. Turn the tray and roast for a further 10 minutes. Keep all the vegetables warm in a low oven.

6 To make the dressing, carefully remove the skin from the Camembert and cut the cheese into small cubes. Place in a small saucepan with the crème fraîche and melt over a very gentle heat for 3-4 minutes. Season with pepper and keep warm. Slice the third pear as finely as you can.

7 To serve, place the croutons, vegetables, pears and hazelnuts on 4 plates. Scatter the raw pear and a little watercress over the top. Finally, spoon over the melted Camembert to serve.

■ 855cals; 59g fat, (25.9g sat fat); 24.7g protein; 11.9g fibre; 61.2g carbs; 27.2g total sugars; 1.9g salt

KITCHEN Secret

When you're peeling beetroot, use disposable gloves to prevent it from staining your fingers.

Smoked trout and prawn salad with dill and lemon

No-cook recipes are invaluable in the summer months and this salad by *Jo Pratt* has become a firm favourite – just the ticket for a balmy evening

Serves 4
Prep 45 **Total time** 45 mins, plus cooling
Get ahead Soak the bulgur wheat and make the dressing up to 1 hour ahead

100g bulgur wheat
100g pea shoots or watercress sprigs
250g hot-smoked trout fillets
200g cooked, peeled, tiger prawns
1 large ripe avocado, peeled and sliced
150g radishes trimmed and quartered
6 spring onions, thinly sliced on an angle

For the dressing
5 tbsp extra-virgin olive oil
2 tbsp lemon juice
finely grated zest of ½ lemon
1 tbsp finely chopped gherkins
1 tsp Dijon mustard
2 tbsp chopped dill

1 Put the bulgur wheat in a medium bowl and pour over 200ml of boiling water. Stir and leave for about 30 minutes, until the water has been absorbed by the bulgur wheat. Fluff with a fork and leave to cool.

2 Meanwhile, to make the dressing, mix together all of the ingredients and season well.

3 Mix half of the dressing into the bulgur wheat and set aside.

4 Divide the pea shoots or watercress between four plates (or use a large platter) and scatter over the dressed bulgur wheat.

5 Break the hot-smoked trout into large flakes and divide among the plates, along with the prawns, sliced avocado, radishes and spring onions.

6 Drizzle over the remaining dressing and serve immediately.

■ 426cals; 27g fat (5g sat fat); 29g protein; 3.5g fibre; 22g carbs; 2g total sugars; 0.5g salt

KITCHEN Secret

Hot smoking cooks fish and adds a wonderful flavour to trout and salmon – a great standby ingredient.

Warm Vietnamese-style chicken salad

Full of flavour and freshness, you will make this recipe by **Sarah Randell** time and time again. Try it with griddled prawns or rare beef, too

Serves 4

Prep 20 mins **Total time** 35 mins
Get ahead Make up to the end of step 1 a few hours ahead and cover with damp kitchen paper. Cook the shallots, toast the peanuts and make the dressing ahead, too

1 small carrot
1 spring onion, trimmed
½ cucumber, deseeded
a handful of mangetout
a small handful each of mint
and coriander leaves
1 tbsp rapeseed or vegetable oil,
plus a little extra
3 shallots, thinly sliced
a small handful of salted
peanuts, chopped
4 skinless chicken breast fillets
2 Little Gem lettuces
lime halves, to serve
For the dressing
2 bird eye chillies, deseeded
and finely chopped
1 garlic clove, finely chopped
1½ tbsp soft brown sugar
3 tbsp lime juice
1½ tbsp Thai fish sauce
3 tbsp rice vinegar or water

1 Shred the carrot, spring onion and cucumber into long strips. Halve the mangetout lengthways, and toss everything in a bowl with the mint and coriander leaves.

2 Heat the oil in a frying pan (or wok). Add the shallots and cook, stirring, until golden. Scoop them on to a plate. Add the peanuts to the pan and toss for 2-3 minutes until golden. Set aside with the shallots. Preheat a griddle.

3 Slice the chicken fillets into strips, toss in a little oil and griddle for 2-3 minutes on each side, or until cooked through. Meanwhile, mix all the ingredients together for the dressing. Toss the shredded vegetables with half the dressing.

4 Separate the lettuce leaves and place a few on each plate. Top with the vegetable mixture and griddled chicken. Drizzle with the rest of the dressing. Sprinkle over the shallots and peanuts and serve with the lime halves.

■ 202cals; 7g fat (1g sat fat); 40g protein; 2g fibre; 14g carbs; 12g total sugars; 0.8g salt

KITCHEN *Secret*

Thai fish sauce is used instead of salt to season Vietnamese and Thai recipes.

Crispy tofu salad with ginger

Tofu, or bean curd, is made from soy milk. Here, it's tossed in cornflour before being fried till crispy

Serves 4
Prep 15 mins **Total time** 20 mins

2 medium carrots, trimmed
1 small Chinese leaf
lettuce, shredded
½ x 28g pack mint, leaves
only, roughly chopped
juice and zest of 1 orange
2-3 tsp finely grated root ginger
2 tbsp rice or white wine vinegar
4 tbsp groundnut or sunflower oil,
plus extra for frying
1 x 396g pack tofu
50g cornflour, well seasoned
50g cashew nuts, roughly chopped

1 Peel the carrots into long ribbons with a flat-bladed peeler. Toss with the shredded Chinese leaf lettuce and chopped mint in a large bowl.

2 Mix the orange juice and zest, ginger, vinegar and oil with some seasoning.

3 Drain the tofu and remove as much moisture as you can by patting it with kitchen paper. Cut into 8 x 1cm slices then cut each slice into three. Toss in the cornflour until coated.

4 Heat some oil in a large nonstick frying pan and cook the tofu, in batches, for 4-5 minutes on each side until golden and crisp, setting aside on kitchen paper. Toast the cashew nuts in the pan until golden.

5 Toss the salad with the dressing, then scatter over the tofu and cashew nuts.

■ 338cals; 23g fat (4g sat fat);
13g protein; 3g fibre; 19g carbs;
5g total sugars; 0g salt

ALSO TRY
Peter Gordon's tomato
and cherry salad
In a large bowl, mix 400g **cherry tomatoes**, halved, 275g **cherries**, halved and pitted, 1 small **red onion**, peeled and thinly sliced into rings, and 2 tablespoons **lemon juice**. Lightly season, then leave, covered, in the fridge for at least an hour. After this time, add 3 tablespoons **coriander** leaves to the bowl. Trim and slice 2 medium **fennel bulbs** very thinly. Add the fennel and 1 tablespoon each **extra-virgin olive oil** and **avocado oil** to the salad, toss it all together then eat promptly. **Serves 8**.

■ 53cals; 2.8g fat, (0.4g sat fat);
1g protein; 1.4g fibre; 6.6g carbs;
6.6g total sugars; 0g salt

KITCHEN Secret

Leftover mint? Put a few sprigs in a mug and steep in boiling water for fresh mint tea. Add sugar or honey to taste.

Flamme tart

This tart is an adaptation of a classic from Alsace. All it needs with it is a crisp green salad and a glass of beer. Recipe by *Annie Rigg*

Serves 4
Prep 15 mins **Total time** 45 mins

  1 tbsp olive oil
  1 x 100g pack cubetti di pancetta
  3 medium onions, sliced
  1 fat garlic clove, crushed
  1 x 375g pack ready-rolled
  puff pastry
  200ml crème fraîche
  few small sprigs oregano

1 Preheat the oven to 200°C, fan 180°C, gas 6 and place a baking sheet on the middle shelf to heat.
2 Heat the oil in a large frying pan over a medium heat, add the pancetta and cook until the fat begins to run. Add the onions and cook for a further 10 minutes, stirring occasionally, until beginning to colour. Add the garlic and cook for a further minute.
3 Meanwhile, unroll the pastry and score a border 2cm in from the edges. Transfer the pastry it a second baking sheet, lightly greased, then place on top of the hot baking sheet in the oven and cook for 7-10 minutes.
4 Take the pastry out of the oven and push down the centre with the back of a fork.
5 Season the crème fraîche and spread half of it over the middle of the pastry. Season the onion mixture and spread on top. Dot over the remaining crème fraîche and return to the oven for 15-20 minutes, until the pastry is golden and the filling is bubbling. Sprinkle with the oregano and serve.
■ 680cals; 53g fat, (27g sat fat); 12g protein; 1g fibre; 42g carbs; 6g total sugars; 1.8g salt

ALSO TRY
Mackerel, tomato and mustard tart
Bake the pastry base as for the flamme tart. Meanwhile break 240g **or peppered smoked mackerel fillets** into small chunks, discarding the skin, and cut each of 4 large ripe **tomatoes** into 8 wedges. Mix 1 tablespoon **wholegrain mustard** and 6 tablespoons **crème fraîche** together. Spread the crème fraîche mixture over the centre of the pastry and then scatter the mackerel, tomatoes and 3 tablespoons chopped **parsley** on top. Return the tart to the oven for 15 minutes or until bubbling.
Serves 4.
■ 674cals; 50.3g fat, (20.5g sat fat); 18.4g protein; 1.9g fibre; 36.5g carbs; 5.4g total sugars; 2g salt

KITCHEN *Secret*

Using ready-made pastry makes this tart a doddle. Keep a few packs in the freezer as a standby.

Yotam Ottolenghi

This dish is full of Middle Eastern flavours, including za'atar – a spice mix combining lemony sumac, salt and sesame seeds

Yotam and his business partner Sami Tamimi have four deli-restaurants and a glam West End all-day eatery, Nopi, in London, as well as a mail-order business. Yotam has introduced a whole host of new ingredients to British cooks and the magazine cookery team particularly love Yotam's book *Jerusalem*.

PLENTY BY YOTAM OTTOLENGHI, PUBLISHED BY EBURY PRESS. REPRINTED BY PERMISSION OF THE RANDOM HOUSE GROUP LTD

Aubergine with buttermilk sauce

Serves 4

Prep 20 mins **Total time** 1 hr
Get ahead Make the sauce the day before; chill. Cook the aubergines an hour ahead; serve warm

2 large, long aubergines
75ml olive oil, plus extra to drizzle
1 tsp lemon thyme or thyme leaves, plus a few extra to finish
sea salt flakes
½ pomegranate
1 tsp za'atar or lemon zest
For the buttermilk sauce
75ml buttermilk
50g Greek yogurt
1 tbsp olive oil
½ garlic clove, crushed

1 Preheat the oven to 200°C, fan 180°C, gas 6. Cut the aubergines in half lengthways (keep the stalks attached). Use a small sharp knife to make 4 or 5 parallel incisions in the flesh of each aubergine half, without cutting through the skin. Repeat at an angle to make a diamond pattern.

2 Place the aubergines cut-side up on a baking tray lined with nonstick baking paper. Brush them with the oil until it's all absorbed. Sprinkle over the lemon thyme leaves, some sea salt and pepper, then roast for 35-40 minutes. Remove from the oven and cool.

3 Meanwhile, hold the pomegranate half over a bowl cut-side down. Tap the

pomegranate skin with a rolling pin to knock the seeds into the bowl. Remove any white skin or membrane from the bowl.

4 For the buttermilk sauce, whisk together all of the ingredients with a pinch of salt; check the seasoning. Spoon the sauce over the aubergines without covering the stalks. Sprinkle over the pomegranate seeds, the za'atar or lemon zest and extra thyme. Finish with a drizzle of oil. Serve with a leafy green salad for a light lunch.

■ 193cals; 18g fat (3g sat fat); 2g protein; 3.5g fibre; 5g carbs; 5g total sugars; 0g salt

'A DIFFERENT WAY TO *cook eggs* THAT CAN BE VARIED WITH THE INGREDIENTS YOU HAVE TO HAND'

Turkish baked eggs

These baked eggs are simple and quick to put together. Serve with flatbreads or toasted pitta

Serves 2
Prep 10 mins **Total time** 30 mins

- **1 onion, thinly sliced**
- **1 red pepper, thinly sliced**
- **1 tbsp oil**
- **1 garlic clove, finely chopped**
- **1 red or green chilli, deseeded and diced**
- **½ tsp ground cumin**
- **1 x 230g tin chopped tomatoes**
- **a small handful of flat-leaf parsley, chopped**
- **2 large eggs**

1 Preheat the oven to 200°C, fan 180°C, gas 6. In a large frying pan, soften the sliced onion and pepper, covered, in the oil for 10 minutes.

2 Add the garlic, chilli and cumin to the pan and cook for a further minute. Stir in the tomatoes, season and simmer, covered, for 5 minutes. Add the parsley.

3 Spoon the mixture into 2 ovenproof dishes, making hollows in the top. Break the eggs into the hollows and bake for 20 minutes.

- 210cals; 14g fat (3g sat fat); 11g protein; 4g fibre; 11g carbs; 10g total sugars; 0.4g salt

ALSO TRY
All-day breakfast salad

Pour 2.5cm of boiling water into a small frying pan and bring to a very gentle simmer. Break in 2 large, very fresh **eggs**, leave for 1 minute and then take off the heat. Leave for 10 minutes. Meanwhile, fry 8 rashers **smoked streaky bacon** in a large frying pan until crisp. Leave the fat in the pan, transfer the bacon onto kitchen paper. Halve 6 thin slices of **French stick**. Fry in the bacon fat until golden. Put 12 halved **cherry tomatoes** into a large bowl with 4 handfuls of **salad leaves** and 2 tbsp **French dressing**. Add the bacon, chopped, with the croutons. Toss together, divide between 2 plates and top with the poached eggs. **Serves 2.**

- 600cals; 37.8g fat, (11g sat fat); 28.9g protein; 3g fibre; 38.3g carbs; 5g total sugars; 4.2g salt

KITCHEN Secret

For a Spanish twist, omit the chilli and cumin, and add some chopped, crisp-fried chorizo and a sprinkle of smoked paprika.

Pea, new potato and feta frittata

A summery lunch to serve with a leafy salad. *Brian Glover*'s frittata would also be excellent for a picnic, cut into wedges

Serves 4
Prep 10 mins **Total time** 40 mins
Get ahead Make a few hours ahead and serve at room temperature

2-3 tbsp olive oil
1 large onion, thinly sliced
500g new potatoes, peeled and sliced
1 tsp chopped thyme
150-200g podded peas
a good knob of butter
6 large eggs, beaten
100g feta or goats' cheese, crumbled
a handful of pea shoots

1 Heat 2 tablespoons of the oil in a 23-25cm nonstick frying pan over a medium heat. Add the onion and 2-3 pinches of salt, and stir. Cover, turn down the heat and sweat the onions for 15 minutes, stirring occasionally.

2 Add the potatoes and thyme to the pan and cook, still covered, for 10-12 minutes until the potatoes are just tender, adding the extra oil if they are drying out. Meanwhile, boil the peas in salted water for 4 minutes, then drain.

3 Uncover the pan and turn up the heat until the potatoes start to colour. Add the butter and, when melted, add the peas. Season the eggs and pour into the pan, stirring in the feta and pea shoots. Preheat the grill.

4 Cook the frittata over a medium heat, drawing in the edge with a spatula until the base sets. After 4-5 minutes, when the underside has browned, put the pan under the grill for 2-3 minutes to just set the top.

■ 413cals; 25.1g fat, (8.9g sat fat); 22.1g protein; 4.7g fibre; 25.8g carbs; 4.7g total sugars; 1.3g salt

ALSO TRY
Red pepper and courgette frittata
Heat a little **olive oil** in a 20 x 5cm deep nonstick frying pan. Cook 2 **red peppers**, deseeded and cut into wedges, until softened. Add 1 **red onion**, peeled and sliced, to the pan. Cook for 5 minutes. Add 2 **garlic cloves**, peeled and chopped, and 1 **courgette**, thinly sliced, and cook for a further 5 minutes. Preheat the grill to high. Whisk 6 large **eggs** with 2 tablespoons chopped **fresh parsley**, season and pour into the pan. Cook for 4-5 minutes. Sprinkle with 1 tablespoon freshly grated **parmesan** and grill for 2-3 minutes until set. **Serves 4**.

■ 191cals; 12g fat, (4g sat fat); 15g protein; 2g fibre; 7g carbs; 3.7g total sugars; 0.4g salt

KITCHEN Secret

Frittatas are open-pan omelettes – they are cooked on the hob, then finished under the grill until just set.

Keralan salmon wraps

These wraps by *Anjum Anand* are really quick and very easy – the spices and aromatics have all the flavours of Southern Indian cooking

Serves 4
Prep 20 mins **Total time** 45 mins
Get ahead Make the recipe up to the end of step 2 a day ahead; reheat before adding the salmon

3 tbsp vegetable oil
½ tsp mustard seeds
1 small onion, finely chopped
10g root ginger, peeled and finely chopped
2 large garlic cloves, finely chopped
8 dried curry leaves
1½ tsp ground coriander
¼ tsp turmeric
¼ tsp red chilli powder, or to taste
¾ tsp garam masala
2 small tomatoes, chopped
60g finely grated coconut, fresh or from a block of creamed coconut
1 tsp lemon juice
25g salted roasted peanuts
300g salmon fillet, cut into 2.5cm cubes
a handful of crunchy lettuce leaves
4 wheat tortillas
limes, to squeeze over

1 Heat the oil in a medium nonstick saucepan. Add the mustard seeds. Once they're popping, add the onion and fry for 7-8 minutes until lightly coloured. Add the ginger, garlic and curry leaves, crumbled, and fry until the garlic begins to colour.

2 Stir in the powdered spices and a pinch of salt. Follow with the chopped tomatoes, grated coconut and 200ml water. Bring to the boil, then cover and simmer for 8-10 minutes or until the whole thing becomes a wonderful sauce. Add the lemon juice and peanuts and over-season slightly, as the fish will absorb some of the salt.

3 Add the salmon and, if the pan is dry, a splash of water, then cover and cook over a low heat for 3-4 minutes or until the salmon is cooked through.

4 Place a bed of lettuce along the length of each tortilla. Top with the salmon mixture, add a squeeze of lime juice and roll tightly. Halve to serve.

■ 504cals; 31g fat (13g sat fat); 22g protein; 5g fibre; 37g carbs; 4g total sugars; 0.6g salt

KITCHEN *Secret*

Curry leaves don't taste of curry! They add a wonderful fragrance and a nutty flavour with a hint of lemon.

ANJUM'S NEW INDIAN BY ANJUM ANAND (QUADRILLE, £14.99)

Goats' cheese, tomato and basil quiche

This recipe by **Alex Mackay** from our July 2006 issue proved popular – crème fraîche makes the quiche lighter but still deliciously creamy

Serves 6-8
Prep 30 mins, plus resting
Total time 1 hr 35 mins
Get ahead Line the tin with the pastry and freeze or refrigerate up to 2 days ahead

- 1 small onion, finely chopped
- 2 garlic cloves, finely chopped
- 1 tbsp extra-virgin olive oil
- 100g young-leaf spinach, chopped
- 50g soft Welsh goats' cheese
- 40g white breadcrumbs
- 200 SunBlush tomatoes

For the pastry
- 50g unsalted butter, at room temperature
- 150g soft Welsh goats' cheese
- 200g plain flour, plus extra for dusting

For the filling
- 2 large eggs and 2 large egg yolks
- 300ml half-fat crème fraîche
- 50g grated parmesan
- small handful basil leaves

1 For the pastry, mix the butter and goats' cheese together until smooth – this can be done in a bowl with a spatula or in a food processor. Add the flour, 1 tablespoon cold water, 1 teaspoon salt and 1 teaspoon coarsely ground black pepper, and mix to a smooth dough. Flour your hands and flatten the dough to a 20cm circle, wrap in clingfilm and refrigerate for 40 minutes before rolling.

2 Meanwhile, in a large shallow pan, gently cook the onion and garlic in the olive oil for 6-7 minutes, until soft. Add the spinach, raise the heat and fry for 2 minutes, until wilted. Transfer to a bowl and leave to cool. When cool, break up the goats' cheese and stir it into the mixture with the breadcrumbs. Season, then set aside.

3 To make the filling, beat the eggs and yolks together with the crème fraîche. Season, then set aside. Preheat the oven to 220°C, fan 200°C, gas 7.

4 Lightly oil a 4cm deep, 23cm round, loose-bottomed tin. Place a large piece of clingfilm on a work surface. Unwrap the pastry, dust with flour, place it on the clingfilm then cover with a second layer of clingfilm. Roll away from yourself from the centre of the pastry out, turning it 90° after each roll, until you have a 28cm circle. Remove the top layer of clingfilm, then roll the pastry and clingfilm loosely around the rolling pin. Hold the rolling pin over the tart tin and unroll the pastry on to the tin. Discard the clingfilm and ease the pastry into the tin. Trim the edges, prick the base all over with a fork, line the tart shell with baking parchment and fill with baking beans or rice. Put onto a baking sheet and bake on the middle shelf of the oven for 15 minutes, or until golden around the edges.

5 Place the tomatoes in the cooked pastry shell, then scatter over the spinach mixture, pour in the filling and sprinkle over the parmesan. Turn the oven down to 180°C, fan 160°C, gas 4, bake for 30 minutes, then turn off the oven and leave for a further 10 minutes. Remove the quiche from the tin and slide off the base on to a cooling rack.

6 Top with basil, and slice it using a sharp serrated knife.

■ 407cals; 26.2g fat, (14.2g sat fat); 15.6g protein; 3.1g fibre; 27.3g carbs; 5.2g total sugars; 1.1g salt

KITCHEN Secret

You can bake the quiche in advance and warm it for 5 minutes in a hot oven just before serving.

Simple Midweek Suppers

Recipes

Macaroni cheese with spinach, tomatoes and spring onions

This is a great family favourite – if you fancy something different, ring the changes with one of our three variations

Serves 4-6
Prep 15 mins **Total time** 45 mins

350g macaroni or other
short dried pasta
50g butter
50g plain flour
1 bunch spring onions, trimmed
and finely sliced
1 litre semi-skimmed milk
125g extra-mature cheddar, grated
50g parmesan, grated
1½ tbsp Dijon mustard
200g young leaf spinach
250g cherry, or baby plum
tomatoes, halved

1 Preheat the oven to 200°C, fan 180°C, gas 6. Cook the pasta in boiling, salted water until just tender (it will finish cooking in the oven), then drain.

2 Meanwhile, for the cheese sauce, put the butter, flour, spring onions and milk in a pan and slowly bring to the boil, whisking all the time until it thickens. Simmer for a few minutes and remove from the heat.

3 Season the sauce and stir in the cheddar and half the parmesan until melted, then add the mustard. Stir in the spinach a handful at a time, so it wilts in the sauce.

4 Mix the cooked pasta with the sauce. Tip it into an ovenproof dish (it will need to be about 2.5 litre capacity), scatter over the tomatoes and remaining parmesan and bake for 25-30 minutes until golden.

■ 516cals; 21.2g fat (12.6g sat fat); 23.5g protein; 4.6g fibre; 57.4g carbs; 11.7g total sugars; 1.3g salt

MAKE IT SPECIAL

Cook and drain the pasta. Omit the spring onions from the sauce. Replace the cheddar and parmesan in the sauce with 75g each of crumbled **Stilton** and **goats' cheese** and a ball of **mozzarella**, torn. Omit the tomatoes. Mix the pasta with the sauce. Scatter with **walnut pieces** and 50g grated parmesan before baking.

MAKE IT HEALTHIER

Cook and drain the pasta. Use skimmed milk and omit the butter in the sauce. Omit the cheddar and parmesan. Mix the pasta with the sauce. Top with the tomatoes, 50g of grated **Grana Padano**, some chopped **parsley** and 4 tablespoons of **breadcrumbs** before baking.

GO MEATY

Cook and drain the pasta. Make the sauce and mix with the pasta. Dry-fry 150g of chopped **streaky bacon** until starting to crisp, add 150g of sliced **chestnut mushrooms** and soften. Stir through 1 tablespoon chopped **sage**, cook for 30 seconds, then add to the sauce and pasta. Omit the spinach. Scatter with the tomatoes and parmesan, and bake.

KITCHEN *Secret*

Get ahead and freeze the macaroni cheese – defrost thoroughly before cooking and cook until golden and bubbling.

Madhur Jaffrey

Beat the takeaway and make your own! Serve Madhur's easy version of this Indian classic with basmati rice or green lentils

Madhur Jaffrey was born in Delhi but moved to London to study drama. She missed Indian homecooked meals, so asked her mother to send her recipes. Her love of food grew and her first cookbook was published in 1973, followed by a TV series. She has written more than 15 books and is regarded by many as the first to introduce Indian recipes to the UK.

'USING A BLENDER HELPS MAKE THE *ginger-garlic paste* QUICKLY'

Easy chicken korma

Serves 8
Prep 30 mins **Total time** 1 hr 5 mins
Get ahead Can be made up to
2 days ahead

**8cm piece root ginger, peeled
and coarsely chopped
8-10 garlic cloves, peeled and
coarsely chopped
4 tbsp vegetable oil
3 bay leaves
1 cinnamon stick
12 cardamom pods
8 cloves
½ tsp cumin seeds
2 onions, finely chopped
2 tbsp ground coriander
2 tbsp ground cumin
2 x 400g tins plum tomatoes,**
**chopped (reserve the juice)
8 chicken breasts in largish chunks
or 16 bone-in thighs, skinless
½-1 tsp hot chilli powder
4 tbsp single cream**

1 Put the ginger, garlic and 3-4
tablespoons water in a blender or
mini chopper. Blend together until
you have a smooth paste.
2 Pour the oil into a casserole and set
over a high heat. When very hot, put
in the bay leaves, cinnamon stick,
cardamom, cloves and cumin seeds.
Stir, then add the chopped onions.
Stir-fry for 3-5 minutes or until the
onions turn a brownish colour.
3 Add the paste from the blender, the
ground coriander and ground cumin,
and fry for a further minute. Pour in
the chopped tomatoes along with
their juice and fry for another minute.
4 Next, add the chicken, chilli powder
and ½ teaspoon salt. Bring to the boil,
then partially cover, reduce the heat
to medium and cook for 15 minutes,
turning the chicken now and then.
5 Remove the cover, add the single
cream and cook for another 7-10
minutes or until the sauce has
thickened and the chicken is cooked
through. Stir gently as you do this.
Check the seasoning before serving.

■ 253cals; 8.7g fat (2.1g sat fat);
37.6g protein; 1.6g fibre; 5.8g carbs;
5g total sugars; 0.34g salt

Gnocchi with artichokes, rocket and almond pesto

Gnocchi are little dumplings, usually made of potato. They are a useful alternative to pasta and cook in minutes

Serves 4
Prep 10 mins **Total time** 20 mins
Get ahead Make the rocket and almond pesto a few hours ahead

1 x 200g pack chargrilled
artichokes in oil, drained
(reserve the oil)
750g fresh gnocchi
½ x 70g bag **rocket leaves**
For the rocket and almond pesto
75g blanched almonds
½ x 70g bag **rocket leaves**
1 **garlic clove**, crushed
50g **parmesan** or other Italian
hard cheese, finely grated,
plus extra to serve
100ml **extra-virgin olive oil**
¼ tsp **sea salt**

1 First, make the rocket and almond pesto. In a dry frying pan, lightly toast the almonds for a couple of minutes, taking care not to burn them. Set aside to cool, then transfer to a food processor with the rocket, the garlic, cheese, olive oil and ¼ teaspoon of sea salt. Whiz to a semi-smooth paste.

2 Heat 1-2 tablespoons of the reserved oil from the artichokes in a large frying pan. Add the gnocchi and toss gently over a medium-high heat for 6-8 minutes until lightly golden. Add the artichokes and rocket pesto to the pan and mix to combine. Remove from the heat and stir the remaining rocket leaves through the gnocchi. Serve sprinkled with a generous grating of cheese.

■ 678cals; 38.9g fat (6.8g sat fat); 16.6g protein; 7.2g fibre; 61.1g carbs; 2.8g total sugars; 3.5g salt

ALSO TRY
Gnocchi with pea shoots, beans and lemon

Preheat the grill on a high setting. Bring a pan of salted water to the boil. Drop 1kg bags **gnocchi**, 250g **tenderstem broccoli**, halved, and 300g frozen **soya beans** or podded **broad beans** into the water. Bring back to the boil and simmer for 2-3 minutes, drain and tip into an ovenproof dish. Stir in 4 tablespoons grated **pecorino**, the zest of 1 large **lemon**, 5-6 tablespoons chopped **basil** and 6 tablespoons **half-fat crème fraîche**, then scatter with 250g **mozzarella**, torn into pieces. Grill for 5-6 minutes or until bubbling and golden. Top with 4 handfuls of **pea shoots** and drizzle with a little **olive oil** before serving. **Serves 4**.

■ 799cals; 29g fat (14g sat fat); 39.3g protein; 10.3 fibre; 87g carbs; 2.1g total sugars; 3.5g salt

KITCHEN
Secret

When boiling gnocchi, you can tell when they are cooked as they will rise to the surface of the water.

Sweet and sour pork

This fresh-tasting version of the classic dish is so much better than any you'll find in a Chinese takeaway

Serves 4
Prep 20 mins **Total time** 40 mins

2 tbsp soy sauce
2 tbsp rice vinegar (or
white wine vinegar)
2 tbsp tomato purée
1 tbsp caster sugar
2 tsp toasted sesame oil
2 tsp cornflour
150ml chicken stock (or water)
1 tbsp groundnut or vegetable oil
500g pork fillet, trimmed
and cubed
2 mixed peppers, deseeded
and cubed
1 bunch of spring onions,
trimmed and chopped
5cm piece root ginger, peeled
and thinly sliced
1 large garlic clove, thinly sliced
1 x 400g pack prepared and cubed
fresh pineapple
noodles, to serve

1 In a bowl, mix together the soy sauce, rice vinegar, tomato purée, sugar, sesame oil, cornflour and stock or water. Set aside.
2 Heat the oil in a wok or large frying pan and when really hot, add the pork and stir-fry for 5 minutes until coloured all over.
3 Add the peppers and spring onions, and stir-fry for a further 5 minutes until softened. Stir in the ginger and garlic and cook for another minute.
4 Stir in the sauce, then let it simmer for a couple of minutes or until the pork is cooked through. Add the pineapple and any juices in the pack and heat through. Serve with noodles.
■ 329 cals; 10g fat (3g sat fat); 29g protein; 4g fibre; 33g carbs; 21g total sugars; 1.6g salt

ALSO TRY
Sweet and sour turkey
Cook 150g **long-grain rice** according to the packet instructions. Put 1 tablespoon **soy sauce** in a bowl, stir in 200g diced **turkey**. In a frying pan, heat 2 tablespoons **sunflower oil** and stir-fry the turkey for 3-4 minutes, with 1 **carrot**, peeled and cut into thin strips and ½ **red or green pepper**, deseeded and cut into thin strips. Add ½ bunch sliced **spring onions** and a peeled and crushed **garlic clove**. Fry for a minute, then add ½ x 227g tin **pineapple pieces** and the juice from the tin, 1 tablespoon **ketchup** and 1 tablespoon **soy sauce**. Bubble for 1-2 minutes. Add a squeeze of **lemon juice** to taste. Serve with the rice. **Serves 2**.
■ 550cals; 12.6g fat (1.7g sat fat); 39.1g protein; 3.4g fibre; 71.8g carbs; 15.9g total sugars; 3.1g salt

KITCHEN *Secret*

Prepare stir-fry ingredients before you start cooking so they're ready to add to the hot wok as you need them.

'A BOWL FULL OF STEAMING MUSSELS PACKED *with flavour* FOR SUPPER'

Mussels with chorizo and manzanilla

This recipe by *Sarah Randell* makes a hearty supper for four. Once bought, store mussels in the fridge and eat them the same day

Serves 4
Prep 15 mins **Total time** 30 mins

2kg prepared mussels
1 tbsp olive oil
200g chorizo, diced
2 fat garlic cloves, sliced
1 heaped tsp smoked paprika
100ml manzanilla sherry, or dry white wine
2 tbsp thyme leaves
8 slices of ciabatta
300ml single cream
juice of 1 small lemon, plus wedges, to serve
flat-leaf parsley leaves, chopped, to serve

1 Rinse the mussels in cold water and discard any that don't close when given a sharp tap with a knife. Drain the mussels in a colander.

2 Heat the oil in a large deep pan. When sizzling, add the chorizo and fry for 3-5 minutes or until coloured at the edges. Add the garlic and smoked paprika and fry for a further minute or so.

3 Pour the sherry or wine into the pan and bubble for a minute. Stir in the thyme, then tip in the cleaned mussels.

Stir the mussels to coat them in the cooking liquid and cover with a tight-fitting lid. Cook over a medium heat for 5-7 minutes or until all the mussels have opened (discard any that haven't). Meanwhile, griddle or toast the ciabatta.

4 Pour the cream into the pan and bring to simmering point. Stir in the lemon juice and ladle the hot mussels and the cooking liquid into deep warm bowls.

5 Scatter with chopped flat-leaf parsley and serve with lemon wedges and the hot ciabatta.

■ 649cals; 34.3g fat (15g sat fat); 39.6g protein; 2g fibre; 37.8g carbs; 6g total sugars; 2.8g salt

ALSO TRY
Moules Normande

Omit the oil, chorizo and smoked paprika. Instead, fry a finely sliced **leek** and the garlic in a generous knob of **butter** for 8-10 minutes until softened. Replace the sherry with **dry cider**. Add the thyme, but use **double cream** in place of the single cream and omit the lemon. **Serves 4.**

■ 708cals; 48.3g fat, (27.2g sat fat); 30.2g protein; 2.7g fibre; 35.7g carbs; 4.1g total sugars; 2.1g salt

KITCHEN *Secret*

To prepare mussels, use a stiff brush to scrape away any barnacles and pull away any frondy 'beards' with a small sharp knife.

'A HINT OF FRAGRANT SPICE TAKES *succulent lamb* TO NEW HEIGHTS'

Lamb chops with garlic and spinach pilaf

We are great fans of **Ruth Watson**, who wrote recipes for the magazine from its launch in September 1993. Enjoy this favourite

Serves 2 generously
Prep 15 mins, plus resting
Total time 40 mins

1 whole garlic head, split into separate cloves
1 tbsp olive oil, plus a little extra
1 tsp each ground cumin and ground coriander
a pinch of hot chilli powder
225g basmati rice, rinsed and drained
450ml hot chicken or vegetable stock
1 fresh or dried bay leaf
3 medium tomatoes, deseeded and roughly chopped
200g young-leaf spinach, rinsed and drained
a handful of fresh parsley, leaves chopped
4 lamb loin chops

1 Bring a pan of water to the boil and add the unpeeled garlic cloves. Boil for 3-4 minutes to blanch, then drain them in a sieve and run under cold water before peeling. Heat the tablespoon of oil in a wide nonstick pan over a medium heat. When hot, add the spices and fry for 1 minute, stirring constantly, then add the rice. Pour in the stock, stir, and add the peeled garlic, bay leaf, tomatoes and some seasoning. Cover the pan, increase the heat and bring to a boil. Stir, then reduce the heat and slowly simmer the rice, covered, for 13-15 minutes.

2 Meanwhile, heat a large wok over a medium heat, then pile in the still-damp spinach and some salt. Cook until the leaves begin to wilt, tossing them constantly with tongs or salad servers.

3 When the rice is just tender and looks pretty dry, stir in the spinach and parsley. Remove the pan from the heat and place a clean folded tea towel under the lid. Leave the pilaf to rest for 10 minutes in a warm place. Fluff the pilaf with a fork to serve.

4 Meanwhile, heat a griddle over a medium-high heat. Oil the lamb chops sparingly, then season. When the griddle is smoking hot, put on the chops and griddle for 3 minutes. Lower the heat, turn the chops and cook for a further 4-8 minutes, depending on thickness and how pink you like your lamb.

■ 783cals; 19.3g fat, (6.2g sat fat); 42.5g protein; 4.8g fibre; 89.3g carbs; 5.9g total sugars; 1.2g salt

KITCHEN
Secret

Basmati is a high-quality long grain rice – the grains don't break up when cooked and it has a sweet aroma and nutty flavour.

Butterflied chicken with chilli aioli

Butterflying chicken breasts means they cook more quickly and evenly. Recipe by *James Ramsden*

Serves 4
Prep 15 mins **Total time** 25 mins
Get ahead Make the aioli a few hours in advance; chill

> 4 skinless chicken breasts
> oil, for griddling
> 200ml groundnut or other flavourless oil
> 2 large egg yolks
> 1-2 red chillies, deseeded and finely chopped
> 2 tbsp finely chopped parsley
> 1 garlic clove, crushed
> a squeeze or two of lemon juice

1 To butterfly the chicken breasts, lay one on a chopping board and, holding it down with the flat of your hand, cut horizontally through the breast, taking care not to cut all the way through. Open the breast so it lays flat, resembling a butterfly. Repeat with the other chicken breasts.

2 Season the chicken on both sides and rub with a little oil. Cook on a hot griddle for 3-4 minutes on each side.

3 Meanwhile, for the aioli, very slowly whisk the oil into the egg yolks until it emulsifies into a smooth sauce. Mix in the chilli, parsley, garlic, lemon juice and some seasoning. If the aioli is a bit thick, add a little water to loosen. Set aside.

4 Remove the chicken from the pan and leave to rest for a few minutes before serving with the aioli and a salad.
Note: this recipe contains raw/partially cooked eggs.

■ 520cals; 41g fat (8.6g sat fat); 37.4g protein; 0g fibre; 0g carbs; 0g total sugars; 0.24g salt

KITCHEN *Secret*

When griddling, it's best to oil the food, rather than the griddle pan, to avoid excessive smoking while you cook.

ALSO TRY
Persian-style chicken
Slice 4 skinless **chicken breasts** into strips and toss with 2 teaspoons each **ground cinnamon** and **ground cumin**, 1 teaspoon **paprika**, the zest of 2 small **lemons**, 2 tablespoons **vegetable oil** and a pinch of salt in a bowl, rubbing the spice mix into the chicken. Preheat a griddle pan and griddle the chicken for 2-3 minutes on each side or until cooked. Toss 1 soft **round lettuce**, leaves separated, with 2 tablespoons **pomegranate molasses** and 2 tablespoons water. Divide the lettuce between two plates, add the chicken, scatter over 4 tablespoons **pomegranate seeds**, 2 tablespoons chopped **walnuts**, 2 trimmed and chopped **spring onions** and 4 tablespoons chopped fresh **coriander**. Drizzle with **low-fat natural yogurt**. **Serves 4.**

■ 301cals; 13g fat (2g sat fat); 38g protein; 1g fibre; 9g carbs; 8g total sugars; 0.3g salt

Antonio Carluccio

A tasty, indulgent and warming risotto from the popular Italian cook and writer

Antonio Carluccio has been cooking authentic Italian food for over 50 years and has taught us much about Italian eating. He was born in Amalfi but, luckily for us, moved to London in the 1970s. We always look forward to magazine photo shoots with Carluccio – his warmth and enthusiasm for good food and recipes is infectious.

Risotto with saffron and sausage

Serves 4
Prep 10 mins **Total time** 45 mins

**1.5 litres chicken or
vegetable stock
300g pork sausages
a good pinch of saffron threads
1 onion, finely chopped
75g unsalted butter
75ml dry white wine
350g risotto rice
50g parmesan, grated**

1 Bring the stock to the boil and keep it simmering in a pot on the stove, next to where you are making the risotto.

2 Remove the sausage skins and break the meat into pieces. Toast the saffron strands in a dry pan for a few seconds, but be careful not to burn them.

3 In a large shallow pan, fry the onion in half the butter, then add the sausagemeat and cook for about 10 minutes, stirring frequently. Add the wine and cook to let it evaporate for a couple of minutes before pouring in the rice.

4 When the rice is coated with butter and is starting to stick to the bottom of the pan, begin adding the hot stock in ladlefuls. Start stirring and, as soon as the first lot of liquid is absorbed, add some more, but not enough to drown it. After about 10 minutes, add the saffron and salt and pepper.

5 Continue adding the stock and, after a further 15 minutes of stirring and adding stock, taste a grain of rice to check if it is al dente.

6 When the rice is ready, stir in the remaining butter and half the parmesan. Serve with the rest of the cheese scattered over.

■ 792cals; 33.8g fat (17.7g sat fat); 21.5g protein; 0.5g fibre; 71g carbs; 2.6g total sugars; 2.7g salt

'NOTHING BEATS A STIR-FRY FOR A *super-speedy* SUPPER'

Teriyaki prawn and mushroom stir-fry

This simple stir-fry is delicious with some thick udon noodles or steamed rice to soak up the tangy sauce

Serves 4
Prep 5 mins **Total time** 25 mins

- 10 tbsp cashew nuts
- 2 tbsp oil
- 450g raw jumbo king prawns
- 3 garlic cloves, finely sliced
- 2 tbsp peeled and finely chopped root ginger
- 2 x 350g packs mushroom stir-fry mix
- 6 tbsp teriyaki sauce
- 1 x 200g pack baby leaf spinach

1 Gently toast the cashews in a dry wok (or large frying pan) on a low heat for a few minutes until golden; remove and set aside.
2 Heat the oil in the wok and fry the prawns on a high heat for 3-4 minutes or until they are almost cooked through.
3 Transfer the prawns to a plate. Add the garlic and ginger to the wok and fry for a minute more.
4 Next, add in the mushroom stir-fry mix, pour over the teriyaki sauce and fry for 4-5 minutes, tossing, until the mushrooms are cooked. Return the prawns to the wok with the spinach and toss over the heat to wilt the spinach, then serve scattered with the nuts.
- 516cals; 31.9g fat (5.2g sat fat); 31.8g protein; 6.7g fibre; 24.8g carbs; 18g total sugars; 2.4g salt

FOR A VEGGIE VERSION
At step 2, replace the king prawns with 300g frozen **Quorn chicken-style pieces**, fried on a medium heat for 7-8 minutes, before adding the garlic and ginger. Replace the mushroom stir-fry mix with 2 x 140g packs **exotic mushrooms**, larger ones torn into pieces, and 2 x 175g packs **baby corn**, halved.
- 424cals; 27.1g fat (4.9g sat fat); 22.5g protein; 6.4g fibre; 22.3g carbs; 15.6g total sugars; 2.6g salt

MAKE IT MEATY
Replace the king prawns with 400g **sirloin steak**, trimmed and cut into thin strips, and add a finely sliced, deseeded **red chilli** with the garlic and ginger. Use 400g chopped **tenderstem broccoli** instead of the mushroom stir fry and the spinach, add 3 tablespoons water along with the teriyaki sauce, and cover and steam for a few minutes until the broccoli is tender.
- 586cals; 36.2g fat (7.3g sat fat); 38.5g protein; 8.7g fibre; 25.8g carbs; 18.7g total sugars; 1.9g salt

KITCHEN *Secret*

If you're using frozen prawns, defrost them in a sieve under cold running water for 1-2 minutes before cooking.

Beany squash and leek stew

A vegetarian stew that is full of colour and flavour – serve with some crusty bread for a satisfying meat-free meal

Serves 4
Prep 10 mins **Total time** 40 mins
Get ahead Make up to 2 days ahead; the stew can also be frozen

1 tbsp olive oil
500g extra-trimmed leeks, cut into 1-2cm slices
2 garlic cloves, chopped
1 sprig of rosemary
1 butternut squash (about 900g), peeled, deseeded and cut into bite-size chunks
juice and zest of 1 small orange
750ml vegetable stock
a pinch of dried crushed chilli flakes
1 x 410g tin cannellini beans, drained and rinsed

1 Heat the oil in a casserole. Add the leeks, garlic and rosemary, cover and cook over a low heat until the leeks are soft, stirring occasionally.
2 Add the squash, orange juice and zest, stock and chilli flakes. Cover and bring to the boil. Cook for about 15 minutes until the squash is tender.
3 Add the beans and cook for a further 5 minutes.
4 Season and remove the rosemary sprig. Using a fork, mash a quarter of the squash pieces against the side of the pan to thicken the sauce.
5 Ladle the stew into bowls and serve with crusty bread.

■ 246cals; 4g fat (1g sat fat); 9g protein; 14g fibre; 33g carbs; 17g total sugars; 1g salt

ON THE SIDE
Garlic mushroom, spinach and mozzarella bruschetta
Preheat the grill to high. Mix one crushed fat **garlic clove** with 1 tablespoon **olive oil** and 1 tablespoon **butter**, and brush or dot over 16 mini **portabella mushrooms**. Season and grill for 5 minutes. Lightly drizzle 4 slices **country-style bread** with a little oil on both sides and grill for 2-3 minutes on each side. Tip 100g **young-leaf spinach** onto a baking tray and toss with the mushrooms. Scatter 125g torn **buffalo mozzarella** on top of the mushrooms and spinach and grill until the cheese melts and the spinach wilts. Top each slice of bread with a quarter of the mushroom mixture and drizzle over any juices. Sprinkle with some chopped **red chilli** and **shredded basil**. **Serves 4**.
■ 329cals; 19.7g fat (7.8g sat fat); 13.9g protein; 4.3g fibre; 24g carbs; 1.9g total sugars; 1.1g salt

KITCHEN
Secret

Also try this recipe with lentils. Add 1 x 400g tin drained green lentils, instead of the beans.

Spicy Asian salmon parcels

The salmon, baked in foil, steams in its juices. Trout fillets work well in this dish, too. Recipe by *Sarah Randell*

Serves 2
Prep 10 mins **Total time** 25 mins

400g pack fresh egg noodles
2 pak choi
2 skinless salmon fillets
2 tsp peeled and grated root ginger
1 red chilli, deseeded and
finely sliced
3 tbsp toasted sesame oil
soy sauce, to serve

1 Pre-heat the oven to 180°C, fan 160°C, gas 4. Divide the egg noodles between 2 large pieces of kitchen foil and place on a baking tray.
2 Cut the pak choi into thin wedges and divide between each pile of noodles, top with a skinless salmon fillet.
3 Scatter each with a teaspoon of the ginger and half the chilli. Drizzle the toasted sesame oil over the fish.
4 Fold the foil over and pinch the edges together to make a parcel. Bake for 15 minutes. Serve hot, drizzled with soy sauce.

■ 567cals; 34.8g fat (5.6g sat fat); 37.5g protein; 4.4g fibre; 25.7g carbs; 1.8g total sugars; 0.6g salt

KITCHEN Secret

Not a fan of oily fish? Use strips of skinless chicken breast or thick haddock fillets instead of the salmon.

ALSO TRY
Crispy cod burritos

Preheat the oven to 150°C, fan 130°C, gas 2. Tip 1 x 128g bag **tempura batter mix** into a bowl and add a pinch of **dried chilli flakes**. Whisk in 150ml of cold water until smooth. Add 300g skinless, boneless **cod fillet**, cut into 2cm-wide pieces, season, add to the batter and turn to coat. In a deep pan heat 5cm of sunflower oil to 180°C, or when a small cube of bread turns golden in 60 seconds. Fry the fish in batches for 4-5 minutes or until crisp, turning occasionally. Drain on kitchen paper. Meanwhile, wrap 8 plain **flour tortillas** in foil and warm in the oven for 10 minutes. Divide the fish among the tortillas with **avocado** slices and **tomato** wedges. Add fresh **coriander**, a pinch of **chilli flakes**, a squeeze of **lime** and a dollop of **soured cream**, before serving. **Serves 4**.

■ 761cals; 26g fat (7g sat fat); 27g protein; 6g fibre; 99g carbs; 4g total sugars; 2g salt

Chilli bean meatballs

Turn ordinary mince into something special with a few extra ingredients and spices. Recipe by *Tamsin Burnett-Hall*

Serves 4
Prep 15 mins **Total time** 45 mins

1 tbsp sunflower oil
1 large onion, peeled and finely chopped
1 red and 1 green pepper, deseeded and diced
¼-½ tsp hot chilli powder, plus extra for sprinkling
½ tsp ground cumin
1 x 390g carton chopped tomatoes
300ml beef stock
400g beef mince
50g fresh breadcrumbs
1 x 410g tin kidney beans, drained and rinsed
225g basmati rice
1 x 150ml pot soured cream

1 Heat the oil in a casserole and fry two-thirds of the onion with the peppers for 5 minutes until golden. Stir in the chilli powder and cumin and cook for 30 seconds, then add the chopped tomatoes and stock. Simmer uncovered for 10 minutes.

2 Meanwhile, mix the remaining onion with the beef mince, breadcrumbs and some seasoning. Shape into 20 meatballs.

3 Brown the meatballs in a nonstick frying pan. Add the browned meatballs to the sauce, along with the kidney beans, and simmer, covered, for 15 minutes.

4 Meanwhile, cook the rice according to pack instructions. Season the meatballs and sauce, and serve on a bed of rice with soured cream and a sprinkling of chilli powder.

■ 685cals; 28g fat (12g sat fat); 34.5g protein; 9g fibre; 76g carbs; 13g total sugars; 1.3g salt

ALSO TRY
A simple Bolognese
Heat 2 tablespoons of **oil** in a deep-sided pan. Brown 500g **beef mince**, 500g **pork mince** and 4 chopped **bacon rashers** in batches, transferring to a bowl as they are ready. Next, add 2 chopped **onions**, 2 chopped **carrots**, 2 chopped **courgettes**, 2 chopped **celery** sticks and 150ml of water. Stir, bring to a simmer, then cover and cook gently for 10 minutes. Remove the lid, stir in 2 tablespoons of **tomato purée** and 125ml **red wine**, and bubble for 5 minutes. Return the browned meat to the pan and stir in 800g chopped **tomatoes**, a strip of **orange peel** and 600ml **beef stock**. Simmer, partially covered, for 1 hour, giving it a stir now and then. Serve with **pasta**, sprinkled with **basil** and **parmesan**. **Serves 8.**

■ 368cals; 21.3g fat (7.8g sat fat); 31.7g protein; 2.8g fibre; 7.5g carbs; 6.8g total sugars; 1g salt

KITCHEN
Secret

Go Italian! Replace the cumin with dried oregano and add 1 tbsp chopped parsley. Use cannellini beans instead of kidney beans. Serve with grated parmesan.

Tagliatelle with prawns, Parma ham and parsley

Theo Randall is a master of pasta and this recipe has a wonderful combination of salty ham with sweet prawns and lots of parsley

Serves 4
Prep 20 mins **Total time** 35 mins

75g unsalted butter
1-2 fat garlic cloves, finely sliced
125g Parma ham, cut into strips 1cm wide
350g peeled raw jumbo king prawns, halved lengthways
1 green chilli, deseeded and finely chopped
400g fresh or dried tagliatelle
6 tbsp chopped flat-leaf parsley
sea salt

1 Melt the butter in a large frying pan, add the garlic and Parma ham and cook gently for 2-3 minutes.
2 Turn up the heat, add the prawns and chilli and cook for 3 minutes, until the prawns are pink. Taste to check the seasoning, but be aware that Parma ham can be quite salty once it's cooked.
3 Meanwhile, cook the tagliatelle in a large pan of boiling salted water for about 3 minutes until al dente, then drain, reserving a little of the cooking water.
4 Add the tagliatelle to the frying pan, together with 3 tablespoons of the cooking water. Toss together with the chopped parsley and some sea salt and freshly ground black pepper and cook over a low heat for about 2 minutes.

■ 624cals; 21.9g fat, (11.9g sat fat); 36g protein; 4.1g fibre; 70.5g carbs; 2.1g total sugars; 2g salt

ALSO TRY
Katie and Giancarlo Caldesi's penne with pancetta, peas and leeks

Cook 315g dried **penne or trofie** in salted boiling water until tender, following the pack instructions. Meanwhile, heat 1 tablespoon of **extra-virgin olive oil** in a large frying pan and fry 1 large **leek**, washed and finely chopped, and 2 x 160g packs **cubetti di pancetta** until golden. Season with freshly ground black pepper. Add 200g frozen **petits pois** to the pasta water and boil for the last 3 minutes of the pasta cooking time. Add 100ml **double cream** to the pancetta and leek mixture and stir together. Drain the pasta and peas, saving 4 tablespoons of the cooking water. Toss the peas and pasta with the sauce, then stir in the reserved cooking water and 25g grated **parmesan**. Serve in warmed bowls. **Serves 4**.

■ 718cals; 39.2g fat, (17.1g sat fat); 28.7g protein; 7.3g fibre; 62.1g carbs; 3.9g total sugars; 2.7g salt

KITCHEN
Secret

Always save a little of the hot water that pasta has been cooked in to add back into the sauce to keep it moist.

Recipes

Roast lemon chicken with sweet and sour onions

Alex Mackay's easy dish is sweet, sour and spicy. If you don't have an ovenproof frying pan, transfer the dish to a shallow tin to braise

Serves 6

Prep 15 mins **Total time** 1 hr 30 mins
Get ahead The dish can be cooked at least a day in advance. Keep chilled, then reheat at 150°C, fan 130°C, gas 2 for 35-40 mins. Can also be frozen

- **1 tbsp vegetable oil**
- **6 chicken legs**
- **zest and juice of 1 orange**
- **zest and juice of 1 lemon**
- **1½ tsp ground cumin**
- **¾ tsp paprika**
- **¾ tsp turmeric**
- **5 medium red onions, cut in half, each half cut into 6 wedges**
- **3 tbsp clear honey**
- **4 tbsp extra-virgin olive oil**
- **300ml chicken or vegetable stock**
- **2 tbsp chopped basil**
- **1 tbsp chopped mint**

1 Preheat the oven to 180°C, fan 160°C, gas 4. Get 1 large (or 2 smaller) ovenproof frying pan very hot with the vegetable oil. Season the chicken with salt and fry for 4-5 minutes skin side down until golden. Drain the fat from the pan, add the orange and lemon juice (reserve the zest), then turn the chicken over.

2 Bring the juice to the boil and reduce by three-quarters until it is sticky and thick. Mix the spices together in a small dish. Turn the chicken legs to coat them with juice, sprinkle with two-thirds of the spices, then transfer to a plate.

3 Turn down the heat to medium and add the onions to the pan with the rest of the spices, the honey and 2 tablespoons of the olive oil. Cover and gently cook over a medium heat for 5-7 minutes until the onions start to soften. Add the stock, bring to the boil and boil furiously for 2 minutes.

4 Put the chicken legs on top of the onions, skin side up. Trickle over the remaining olive oil and braise for 1 hour, uncovered, on the top shelf of the oven. Sprinkle with the citrus zest and herbs just before serving.

■ 638cals; 42g fat, (10.2g sat fat); 47.6g protein; 1.8g fibre; 18.6g carbs; 7.6g added sugar; 0.8g salt

KITCHEN Secret

Chop extra herbs and mix with couscous and seasoning to serve with the chicken.

Basil leaf and Parma ham-wrapped prawns with lemon and basil risotto

This creamy risotto with juicy prawns by **Ruth Watson** is one of our all-time favourite entertaining recipes. It was first published in 1998

Serves 4
Prep 30 mins **Total time** 1 hr 10 mins
Get ahead Prep up to the end of step 1 a few hours ahead, chill

24 large basil leaves
24 raw freshwater or tiger prawns, peeled
1 x 85g pack Parma ham (or sliced pancetta)
For the risotto
1 large lemon
1 litre vegetable stock
40g unsalted butter
2 shallots, peeled and finely chopped
1 large garlic clove, peeled and finely chopped
275g carnaroli or Arborio risotto rice
50ml dry white wine
sea salt
about 2 tbsp roughly chopped fresh basil

1 Wrap a basil leaf around the middle of each prawn, followed by just enough Parma ham to tuck around the prawn in a single layer with a small overlap. Wrap up 3 prawns, then thread them on to a skewer. Try to secure the edges of the ham as you thread them on, but it doesn't matter if they look a bit untidy, as long as they are not falling apart completely. Repeat until all 8 skewers are each loaded with 3 wrapped prawns.

2 You want to get a large oiled griddle or pan burning hot before you start cooking the prawns so start heating up the griddle or pan just before you add the lemon to the risotto.

3 To make the risotto, remove the zest from the lemon and finely chop it, then cut the lemon in half and remove any seeds. Leave both zest and lemon halves to one side at room temperature. In a saucepan, bring the vegetable stock to a gentle simmer and keep it simmering while you are making the risotto.

4 Melt 25g of the butter in a wide saucepan over a low-to-medium heat. Gently fry the shallots and garlic for about 5 minutes, until slightly softened. Now tip in the rice and stir thoroughly for a minute until all the grains glisten. Turn the heat up to medium and pour in the wine. Stir again for a few moments until the liquid has virtually disappeared.

5 Throw some sea salt into the rice and start adding the hot stock, 1-2 ladles at a time, stirring constantly. Adjust the heat to keep the risotto at a simmer, and add only enough liquid to gently bathe the rice, not drown it. As the stock is absorbed, add further ladles of stock, stirring all the time. Continue with this routine for about 20 minutes, then stir in the lemon zest and the juice of half the lemon. Season with a generous amount of black pepper.

6 Carry on stirring, but test a grain of rice with your teeth to see if it is cooked. When it's ready, each individual grain should be just tender, neither soggy nor nutty in the middle. If the stock has been used up before this point is reached, simply add a little more hot water.

7 Put the skewers on to the preheated griddle and cook for a couple of minutes before turning them over and cooking on the other side. When cooked, the Parma ham should be caramelised in patches of golden brown, and any visible prawn meat should look opaque. Once cooked, remove the griddle from the heat while you finish the risotto, but leave the prawns on it.

8 When the risotto is ready, which normally takes about 25 minutes if using carnaroli rice (a little less with Arborio), it should look like a wettish, porridgey mass – not stiff and dry like a pilaf. Remove the pan from the heat and adjust the flavourings, adding more lemon juice if necessary, and seasoning to taste.

9 Finally, stir in the remaining butter and the chopped basil. Divide the risotto between 4 warmed serving plates, perch two skewers per person on top of the rice and serve at once.

■ 449cals; 12.3g fat (6.4g sat fat); 26.1g protein; 0.2g fibre; 51.5g carbs; 0.5g total sugars; 1.4g salt

Italian stuffed roast pork

A mouthwatering take on roast pork that's full of Italian flavours to make a Sunday lunch with a difference

Serves 6

Prep 20 mins **Total time** 2 hrs 10 mins, plus resting

Get ahead Stuff the pork up to a few hours ahead; chill. Return to room temperature before roasting

- 2 tbsp olive oil
- 1 medium leek, white part only, finely chopped
- 2 pork sausages
- 10 sage leaves, finely chopped
- 20g breadcrumbs
- 20g blanched almonds, chopped
- 1 tsp fennel seeds, crushed
- zest and juice of 1 lemon
- 1.5kg boneless loin of pork, skin scored, at room temperature
- 2 tsp sea salt
- 3 fennel bulbs, quartered and sliced, fronds reserved
- 100g cubetti di pancetta
- 200g kale

1 Preheat the oven to 220°C, fan 200°C, gas 7. Heat 1 tablespoon of the oil in a frying pan; add the leek and cook for 8-10 minutes until soft; transfer to a bowl. Squeeze the sausagemeat from the skins and add to the leek. Add the sage, breadcrumbs, almonds, half the fennel seeds and the lemon zest. Season and mix well.

2 Remove any string from the pork and unroll, skin side down, on a clean board. Using a sharp knife, cut into the meat horizontally about two-thirds of the way along (but not all the way through), keeping the knife parallel to the board, to make a pocket. Open the meat out like a book and spread the stuffing into the joint, leaving a 2cm border. Roll up tightly; tie with string.

3 Weigh to calculate the cooking time (see step 4); transfer to a roasting tin. Rub the skin with 1 teaspoon of the oil. Mix the remaining fennel seeds with the sea salt and spread over the scored skin. Roast in the preheated oven for 20 minutes.

4 Meanwhile, in a bowl, toss the fennel with the remaining olive oil and the pancetta; season with black pepper. After 20 minutes, remove the pork from the oven and scatter the fennel mixture into the tin. Reduce the temperature to 160°C, fan 140°C, gas 3; return to the oven for 1 hour 30 minutes (or 25 minutes per 500g) until cooked through. Transfer the pork to a board, cover and leave to rest for at least 20 minutes.

5 Meanwhile, cook the kale in boiling water for 3-4 minutes until tender; drain and add to the tin with the fennel. Toss together, add the fennel fronds and lemon juice and season. Serve with the pork.

■ 461cals; 22g fat (6g sat fat); 61g protein; 4g fibre; 5g carbs; 2g total sugars; 3g salt

KITCHEN *Secret*

Leftover sausages? Combine the meat with cooked onions and breadcrumbs. Shape into meatballs and cook with a simple tomato sauce to go with spaghetti.

Angela Hartnett

Angela's delicious meat-free main course can be made ahead and reheated for easy entertaining

Most well-known for Murano, her own Michelin-starred restaurant in Mayfair, Angela Hartnett also co-runs a restaurant in the New Forest at Lime Wood Hotel. She previously worked closely with Gordon Ramsay, including running the restaurant at the Connaught Hotel. Angela's high-end cooking has an Italian accent but it's her home cooking with favourites such as aubergine Parmigiana, that really reflects her Italian roots.

Aubergine Parmigiana

Serves 8
Prep 20 mins **Total time** 2 hrs 10 mins

200ml olive oil
1 large onion, chopped
2 garlic cloves, crushed
2 x 400g tins plum tomatoes
a pinch of sugar
4 large aubergines
3 x 125g balls buffalo mozzarella,
drained and sliced
1 x 28g pack basil, leaves only
150g parmesan or other Italian-
style hard cheese, freshly grated

1 Put 2 tablespoons of the oil into a medium pan over a low heat. When hot, add the onion and garlic. Cook for 8-10 minutes until soft but not coloured.

2 Add the tomatoes, break up gently with a wooden spoon and add 200ml water. Simmer, uncovered, for 25-30 minutes until thickened. Season with the sugar, salt and freshly ground black pepper. Whiz in a food processor. Press through a sieve into a bowl (discard the seeds and pulp).

3 Cut the aubergines lengthways into 5mm slices and sprinkle with a little salt. Leave for 10 minutes, then pat dry with kitchen paper.

4 Heat some of the remaining oil in a large frying pan. When hot, shallow-fry the aubergine in batches until light golden on both sides, adding more oil as needed. Transfer to a plate lined with kitchen paper. Preheat the oven to 160°C, fan 140°C, gas 3.

5 Spoon a third of the tomato sauce into a 25 x 20cm ovenproof dish. Add a layer of aubergine, overlapping slightly, a layer of mozzarella, then a handful of basil and a sprinkling of parmesan. Repeat twice, seasoning well between each layer. Finish with a layer of aubergine and the remaining cheese.

6 Cook on a baking tray in the oven for 45-50 minutes until a lovely bubbling crust has formed.

■ 403cals; 34g fat (13g sat fat); 17.6g protein; 3.9g fibre; 8g carbs; 6g total sugars; 0.9g salt

South Indian-style beef and broccoli

A recipe that is simple to make and impressive to bring to the table, from Indian food writer and restaurant critic *Roopa Gulati*. Serve with rice

Serves 4
Prep 15 mins **Total time** 25 mins, plus marinating
Get ahead Marinate the beef a couple of hours ahead

- **400g lean sirloin steak, sliced into 1cm thick strips**
- **¾ tsp dried crushed chilli flakes**
- **2 garlic cloves, finely chopped**
- **juice of 1 lime**
- **1½ tsp caster sugar**

For the stir-fry
- **4 tbsp vegetable oil**
- **2 tsp mustard seeds**
- **2 tbsp curry leaves, fresh or dried**
- **1 large red onion, halved and sliced**
- **75g root ginger, peeled and finely chopped**
- **400g tenderstem broccoli, cut into short lengths**
- **2 red chillies, finely chopped**
- **250ml coconut cream**
- **juice of 1 lime**
- **2 tbsp roughly chopped coriander**

1 In a bowl, combine the steak strips with the crushed chilli flakes, garlic, lime juice and sugar, cover and leave to one side for 20 minutes.

2 Using kitchen paper, pat the beef dry, so it will brown quickly. Heat a pan or wok over a high heat and, when hot, add 1-2 tablespoons of the vegetable oil. Stir-fry the beef for 2-3 minutes until brown – do this in 2 or 3 batches. Scoop out the steak, wipe the pan and add the remaining oil.

3 Turn the heat down to medium and toss in the mustard seeds followed by the curry leaves (if using dried leaves, add them with the coconut cream) and fry for about 30 seconds, until they release their aroma. Add the onion and ginger and fry for 2 minutes, stirring continuously.

4 Tip in the broccoli and chilli, and cook until barely tender – another 2-3 minutes. Return the beef to the pan, turn off the heat, then stir in the coconut cream, lime juice and chopped coriander; taste and adjust the seasoning accordingly.

■ 433cals; 30g fat (14g sat fat); 30g protein; 4g fibre; 12g carbs; 7g total sugars; 0.3g salt

ON THE SIDE
Sticky rice with chilli and coconut

Cook 250g **Thai fragrant rice** in plenty of boiling, well-salted water for 10 minutes until tender. Drain well. Meanwhile, toast 2 tablespoons **desiccated coconut** in a dry frying pan for a few minutes or until golden. Stir into the cooked rice with 1 **red chilli**, deseeded and finely chopped, reserving a little of each to scatter over the top. Scatter with a few shredded **basil leaves** just before serving. **Serves 4**

■ 270cals; 5g fat (4g sat fat); 5g protein; 1.4g fibre; 46.8g carbs; 0.5g total sugars; trace salt

KITCHEN *Secret*

Coconut cream is thicker than coconut milk and adds a wonderful richness to dishes.

Pissaladière

A much-loved tart throughout France, this version from **Lorna Wing** proved a hit with our readers. Serve at a summer barbecue, buffet or picnic

Serves 8
Prep 15 mins **Total time** 1 hr 10 mins
Get ahead The tomato topping can be prepared up to 2 days in advance. The pissaladière can be cooked up to 4 hours before serving and reheated in the oven

75ml vegetable oil
750g large onions, sliced
1 bay leaf
a few sprigs of thyme, stalks discarded and leaves chopped, plus a few extra tiny sprigs, to garnish
2 x 50g tins anchovy fillets
185g pitted black olives
1 x 170g tin concentrated tomato purée
thyme leaves, to serve
For the dough
350g strong white bread flour, plus a little extra for kneading
½ level tsp bicarbonate of soda
1½ level tsp cream of tartar
225ml tepid milk

1 To make the topping, put the oil in a large frying pan over a medium heat and add the onions, bay leaf and chopped thyme, stir well and cook for 5 minutes. Cover, reduce the heat to low and cook for 25 minutes, stirring occasionally. Remove the lid, increase the heat and cook the onions for a further 8-10 minutes, until they are meltingly soft and pale golden. Season well, remove from the heat and discard the bay leaf.

2 Drain the anchovy fillets, reserving 1 tablespoon of the oil. Cut the anchovies in half lengthways and leave them to one side. Drain the olives and toss them in the reserved anchovy oil. Season the tomato purée.

3 To make the dough, sieve the flour, bicarbonate of soda, cream of tartar and 1½ level teaspoons of salt together into a medium-sized bowl and, using a wooden spoon, gradually mix in the tepid milk to make a soft dough. Alternatively, put all the dry ingredients into a food processor bowl, mix at high speed for 10 seconds and, with the motor still running, add the tepid milk and continue to blend for approximately 45 seconds, until the mixture forms a soft dough.

4 Preheat the oven to 200°C, fan 180°C, gas 6. Gently knead the dough on a lightly floured surface for 1-2 minutes, until smooth. Now roll it out until it is a little larger than a 30 x 38cm lightly oiled baking sheet. Trim the edges and lift it on to the baking sheet. Prick the dough all over with a fork.

5 Spread the tomato purée on the dough to within 1cm of the edges. Spoon the cooked onions and thyme on top and spread to the edges, too. Then arrange the anchovies in rows to form large diamonds, and put an olive in the centre of each diamond.

6 Bake the pissaladière for 18-20 minutes on the middle shelf of the oven, until the dough is crisp and golden. Sprinkle with the tiny thyme sprigs and serve warm.

■ 341cals; 13.9g fat (2.4g sat fat); 10.5g protein; 5.4g fibre; 42.5g carbs; 9.7g total sugars; 1.9g salt

KITCHEN *Secret*

Pissaladière is also delicious topped with a mass of sliced, roasted peppers.

Szechuan chicken with oriental salad and hot minted potatoes

Simon Hopkinson wrote this recipe for the first issue of the magazine in May 1993, sharing his favourite combination of cold salad and hot potatoes

Serves 4-6
Prep 45 mins **Total time** 1 hr
Get ahead Make the dressing and the peanut sauce a few hours ahead

- **12 small new potatoes, scrubbed or peeled**
- **25g melted butter**
- **12 mint leaves, chopped**
- **225-350g cooked chicken, in strips coriander sprigs to garnish**

For the oriental salad
- **125g rice noodles (pour boiling salted water over, leave for 4 minutes, then drain and cover with cold water until required)**
- **225g bean sprouts**
- **1 large carrot, peeled and sliced lengthways**
- **1 cucumber, peeled, deseeded, cut in half and sliced lengthways**
- **2 x 2.5cm pieces root ginger, peeled, sliced and cut into thin strips**
- **1 red onion, sliced into rings**
- **1 x 31g pack coriander, leaves only**
- **6 sprigs mint, leaves only**

For the salad dressing
- **1 tbsp sesame seeds, toasted**
- **2 tbsp rice vinegar**
- **2 tbsp soy sauce**
- **4 tbsp fish sauce**
- **1 garlic clove, finely chopped**
- **1 tbsp toasted sesame oil**
- **6 tbsp groundnut or other flavourless oil**

For the peanut sauce
- **225g peanut butter, smooth or crunchy**
- **75ml soy sauce**
- **4 tbsp lemon juice**
- **4 tbsp toasted sesame oil**
- **3 small globes stem ginger**
- **2 tbsp stem ginger syrup**
- **6 shakes of Tabasco, or enough to taste**
- **2 garlic cloves**

1 Begin by cooking the potatoes in boiling, salted water until tender. Drain and toss in the butter and mint, then season with pepper and keep warm. For the salad dressing, mix together the sesame seeds, vinegar, soy sauce, fish sauce and garlic in a bowl and then whisk in the oils and set aside.

2 Drain the noodles and place in a large bowl with all the salad ingredients. Mix them thoroughly with your hands. Pour over the dressing, toss lightly and allow the salad ingredients to wilt slightly before serving.

3 Now make the peanut sauce. Put all the ingredients into a blender with 75ml cold water and process to a smooth paste. The desired consistency is one of thick cream; add a little more water if necessary.

4 Finally, divide the oriental salad between 4 or 6 plates. Top with the chicken and spoon over the peanut sauce. Garnish with the coriander. Serve the potatoes separately.

■ 716cals; 46.9g fat (10.1g sat fat); 26.9g protein; 6.9g fibre; 43.8g carbs; 11.7g total sugars; 5.6g salt

KITCHEN *Secret*

Ready-to-use fresh rice noodles work well in this recipe, too

Pork fillet with smoked paprika and piquillo peppers

London-based Spanish chef *Jose Pizarro*'s dish is great for a crowd. Serve with a green salad dressed with an olive oil and sherry vinegar vinaigrette

Serves 8

Prep 20 mins **Total time** 55 minutes, plus overnight marinating

Get ahead This recipe is best started the day before so the pork has plenty of time to marinate. You can prepare the piquillo peppers ahead of cooking the pork, just reheat gently to serve

3 pork fillets, each weighing 500-600g
2 tbsp olive oil, plus extra for drizzling
2 garlic cloves, sliced
1 x 220g jar piquillo peppers, drained and roughly torn (keep the juices from the jar)
1 tbsp chopped parsley

For the marinade

1 tsp sweet smoked paprika, plus extra to sprinkle
3 tbsp olive oil
1 garlic clove, finely chopped
1 tsp dried oregano

1 Mix all the marinade ingredients, adding some freshly ground black pepper. Put the fillets into the marinade and turn them in it. Cover and leave in the fridge overnight.

2 The next day, preheat the grill to medium. Season the fillets with salt and grill them, whole, on a baking tray for 30-35 minutes, turning them often.

3 Meanwhile, heat the 2 tablespoons of olive oil in a frying pan and add the sliced garlic. Cook until it starts to turn golden, then add the peppers and their juices and cook, stirring, for 2-3 minutes. Season and stir in the parsley.

4 Rest the cooked pork for 5 minutes before slicing it. Arrange it on a large platter with the peppers; drizzle with a little extra oil and sprinkle with salt, pepper and extra smoked paprika

■ 316cals; 16.3g fat (3.6g sat fat); 41.2g protein; 1.3g fibre; 2g carbs; 2g total sugars; 0.3g salt

KITCHEN *Secret*

Smoked paprika is made from ground pimiento peppers and adds a smoky spicy flavour to recipes.

Rick Stein

This recipe is a vegetarian winner from Rick. Soaking the cashews gives them a creamy texture and you'll have plenty of curry powder to make the curry again

Rick Stein is the undisputed king of Padstow, a small Cornish fishing village where he owns and runs four restaurants, as well as overseeing two more. He's a familiar face in our homes and on our TV screens, with 16 cookbooks to his name and innumerable television appearances, including his *Far Eastern Odyssey*, which this recipe comes from.

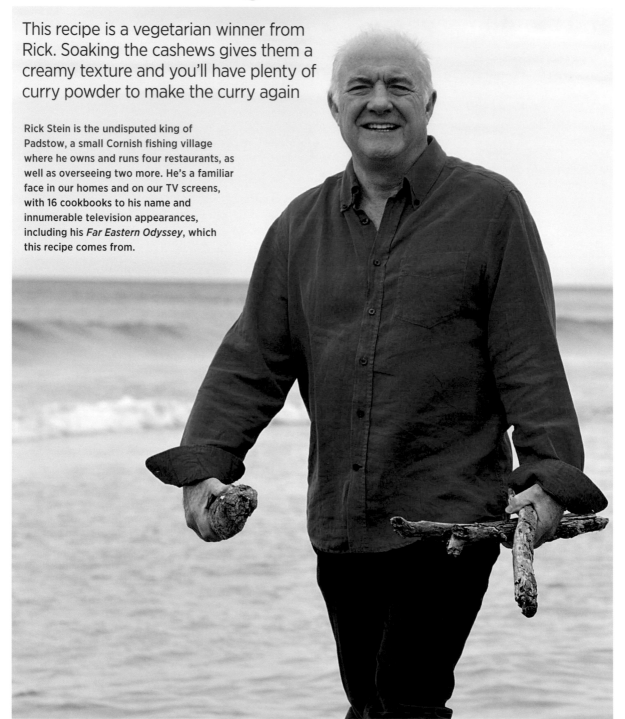

Sri Lankan cashew nut curry

Serves 4-6
Prep 25 mins
Total time 1 hr 40 mins

300g unsalted cashew nuts
2 tbsp coconut or vegetable oil
7.5cm cinnamon stick
1 medium onion, finely chopped
2 fat garlic cloves, crushed
25g root ginger, finely grated
2 green chillies, thinly sliced
½ tsp ground turmeric
400ml coconut milk
2 fat stems lemongrass, cores
finely sliced
4 x 3cm pieces pandan leaf
(optional)
10-12 curry leaves
150g green beans, in 3-4cm pieces
1 tsp jaggery, or light brown sugar
1 tbsp lime juice
a handful of chopped
coriander leaves
For the roasted curry powder
½ tbsp long-grain rice

10g coriander seeds
10g cumin seeds
25g fennel seeds
4cm cinnamon stick
1 tsp fenugreek seeds or ¼ tsp
ground fenugreek
¼ tsp cloves
seeds of 5 cardamom pods
¼ tsp black mustard seeds
½ tsp black peppercorns
1½ dried red chillies

1 Put the cashew nuts into a bowl, cover with boiling water and soak for 30 minutes.

2 For the roasted curry powder, heat a heavy-based frying pan over a medium heat. Add the rice and shake the grains around for about 3 minutes until medium brown in colour. Tip into a bowl, cool. Now do the same to the spices, and then to the dried chillies. Mix the rice, spices and chillies and grind or whiz to a powder. This will make more curry powder than you need but it keeps well.

3 Heat the oil in a medium-sized pan, sizzle the cinnamon stick for a few seconds, then add the onion and garlic and fry gently for 5 minutes until just beginning to brown.

4 Stir in the ginger, green chillies, turmeric, 2 teaspoons of the roasted curry powder, coconut milk, lemongrass, pandan leaf (if using) and curry leaves. Cover and leave to simmer for 20 minutes.

5 Drain the cashew nuts and stir them into the sauce with 150ml of water and ½ teaspoon of salt. Cover and simmer for 20 minutes. Add the beans and cook for a further 10 minutes. Uncover the pan towards the end of cooking to reduce the sauce a little.

6 Stir the jaggery or sugar, lime juice and coriander into the curry and season with salt.

■ 349cals; 28g fat (5.3g sat fat); 9.7g protein; 3.2g fibre; 14.2g carbs; 7.6g total sugars; 0.2g salt

Sausage and fennel lasagne

This is *Katie Caldesi*'s version of a dish she ate in a restaurant in Siena. It takes lasagne to a whole new level

Serves 8
Prep 40 mins **Total time** 1 hr 50 mins
Get ahead Assemble the lasagne, ready to bake, the day before; chill. Cook for 1 hour. It can also be frozen before baking

- 1 x 250g pack dried lasagne sheets
- 1 x 210g pack mozzarella, drained
- 75g finely grated parmesan

For the ragù
- 6 tbsp olive oil
- 1 onion, finely chopped
- 2 garlic cloves, crushed
- 2 x 400g packs Sicilian-style pork sausages
- 1 tbsp fennel seeds, lightly crushed
- 2 bay leaves
- 125ml red wine
- 3 heaped tbsp tomato purée
- 2 x 400g tins peeled plum tomatoes

For the béchamel sauce
- 1 litre milk
- 1 small onion, halved through the root
- 2 bay leaves
- ¼ nutmeg, finely grated
- 75g butter
- 75g plain flour

1 For the ragù, heat the oil in a frying pan and soften the onion and garlic. Remove the sausages from their casings and break up the meat. Stir the fennel seeds and bay leaves into the onions, season, add the sausagemeat and fry for 6-7 minutes until cooked, using a wooden spoon to break it up and stop it from sticking.

2 Add the wine and reduce for a couple of minutes. Add the tomato purée and tinned tomatoes and break them up with a spoon. Leave to simmer for 30 minutes, uncovered. Preheat the oven to 200°C, fan 180°C, gas 6.

3 For the béchamel sauce, put the milk, onion, bay leaves and grated nutmeg in a saucepan, season and bring to a gentle boil. Melt the butter in a small pan and stir in the flour. Cook for a few minutes over a medium heat, stirring constantly, to make a roux. Remove the bay leaves and onion from the milk then add the roux, whisking furiously to avoid lumps. Cook until the sauce thickens, adjust the seasoning to taste and remove from the heat.

4 Spread 2 ladlefuls of the béchamel sauce over the base of a 30 x 20cm ovenproof dish. Add a layer of ragù and top with a layer of lasagne sheets. Thinly slice and layer a third of the mozzarella along with a quarter of the parmesan. Repeat the layers of béchamel, ragù, pasta and cheeses to build up about three layers, finishing with a layer of béchamel.

5 Scatter with the remaining parmesan and bake for 40 minutes until golden and bubbling.

■ 755cals; 49g fat (22g sat fat); 32g protein; 3g fibre; 48g carbs; 13g total sugars; 2.7g salt

KITCHEN *Secret*

Using sausages instead of mince means the ragù is quicker to make than a traditional one.

Moroccan chermoula lamb

Marinating and then barbecuing the lamb makes it deliciously succulent and full of fresh, zingy flavour. A summer sizzler by *David Morgan*

Serves 8
Prep 15 mins **Total time** 45 mins, plus marinating
Get ahead Marinate the lamb the night before; chill. Bring to room temperature before cooking

- 2 x 31g packs coriander, leaves only
- 2 x 28g packs mint, leaves only
- 4 garlic cloves, peeled
- 2 tsp ground cumin
- 2 tsp ground coriander
- 2 tbsp harissa paste
- juice and zest of 1 lemon
- 2 tbsp olive oil
- 1 x 2.5kg leg of lamb, boned and butterflied (ask your butcher to do this for you), or 2 x butterflied lamb legs, approx 750g each

For the yogurt dressing
- 100g preserved lemons, drained and chopped (pips discarded)
- 250g Greek yogurt
- ½ x 28g pack mint, leaves picked and finely chopped

1 Reserve a few coriander and mint leaves to garnish. In a mini processor whiz the remaining coriander and mint leaves with the garlic, cumin, ground coriander, harissa paste, lemon juice and zest and olive oil to a smooth marinade.

2 Place the lamb flat on a board, skin-side up. Score the white fat with a sharp knife, then place the lamb in a large bowl. Pour the marinade over the lamb and rub into the meat on both sides. Cover and chill for at least 4 hours, or overnight, but bring to room temperature before cooking.

3 Light the barbecue. Place the lamb on a barbecue rack and cook over the hot coals for about 15 minutes on each side, basting frequently with any leftover marinade, until the meat is tender and cooked to your liking. Leave to rest for 10 minutes or so before carving.

4 For the yogurt dressing, mix half of the preserved lemon with the yogurt and mint. Garnish the lamb with the reserved mint and coriander leaves and the remaining chopped preserved lemon. Serve with the yogurt dressing.

■ 351cals; 21g fat (9g sat fat); 39.4g protein; 0.1g fibre; 1g carbs; 1g total sugars; 0.9g salt

ALSO TRY
One-pot lamb with olives, tomatoes and spinach

Preheat the oven to 160°C, fan 140°C, gas 3. Heat a little **oil** in a casserole and brown 750g **lamb shoulder** in chunks; transfer it to a plate when it's ready. Soften a sliced **onion**, 2 finely sliced **garlic cloves**, 2 **red peppers** in chunks, and a few sprigs of **rosemary** in the casserole for 5 minutes. Return the lamb, stir in 500ml hot **vegetable stock** and season. Bring to the boil, then cover and transfer to the oven for 1 hour. Stir in 2 x 410g tins **cannellini beans**, drained, 300g **cherry tomatoes** and 100g **pitted olives**; return to the oven for 15 minutes. Stir in 100g **young leaf spinach**, bake for a further 15 minutes. Mix 2 tbsp chopped **parsley** into 150ml **crème fraîche**, serve with the lamb. **Serves 4.**

■ 698cals; 35g fat (11g sat fat); 51.6g protein; 13.9g fibre; 45g carbs; 13g total sugars; 1.5g salt

Potato and celeriac pie

A free-form, or de-constructed vegetarian pie that doesn't require a special tin for baking. Recipe by *Caroline Liddell*

Serves 6
Prep 30 mins **Total time** 1 hr 40 mins
Get ahead Bake the pie ahead and serve it cold with chutneys and pickles

- **900g potatoes**
- **700g celeriac**
- **1 large onion**
- **100g butter**
- **1 x 15g pack chives, snipped**
- **2 tbsp snipped flat-leaf parsley**
- **1 tbsp chopped tarragon leaves**
- **¼ nutmeg, grated**
- **400g puff pastry**

To glaze
- **1 large egg yolk**
- **1 tbsp milk**

1 Preheat the oven to 200°C, fan 180°C, gas 6. Peel the potatoes, celeriac and onion and slice all the vegetables very thinly, no more than 3mm thick. This can be done in a trice using the fine cutting blade in a food processor.

2 Heat the butter in a pan until the froth starts to subside. Tip in all the vegetables and, using a spoon in each hand, toss them in the butter. Continue to cook over a moderate heat for about 8 minutes, tossing the vegetables frequently to make sure they cook evenly, but do not brown.

3 When the vegetables have softened a little but still retain some crispness, transfer them to a large bowl to cool quickly. Add the herbs and grate in the nutmeg, then mix well. Season to taste with salt and pepper, cover with a clean cloth and leave aside until cold.

4 To make the free-form pie, divide the pastry into two pieces, one piece weighing 225g, the other 175g. Roll out the smaller piece to a 25.5cm round and lay it on a greased baking tray. Make an even mound of the cooled vegetable mixture in the centre of the pastry, leaving a clear border 2.5cm wide around the edge. Brush this border with some of the glaze made from the combined egg yolk, milk and ¼ tsp salt. Roll out the remaining pastry to a 30cm round. With the rolling pin, lift the pastry and drape it over the vegetable filling.

5 Using your hands, gently shape the pastry over the mound of filling down over the clear, glazed border, and gently press and seal the two borders together. Leaving a clear 2.5cm edge, trim off any excess pastry with a pair of scissors and either crimp the edges together by pressing with a fork, or pinch together between thumb and forefinger.

6 Glaze the pie with the rest of the egg yolk mix then re-roll any pastry trimming and cut out leaves to decorate the pie. Finally, glaze any decorations and cut a steam hole in the top of the pie.

7 Bake the pie in the centre of the oven for 1 hour. About 15 minutes before the time's up, check to see how the pie is cooking. If it is sufficiently browned, cover loosely with a sheet of foil. When the hour is up, poke a skewer through the steam hole. If the vegetables offer any resistance, continue cooking for a further 15 minutes.

- 533cals; 31.5g fat (16.7g sat fat); 5.3g protein; 8.7g fibre; 28.4g carbs; 4.2g total sugars; 0.55g salt

KITCHEN Secret

Glazing pastry with an 'egg wash' – egg lightly beaten with milk – makes it gorgeously golden.

Scandi-style salmon

Serve this all-in-one bake with crème fraîche mixed with a little horseradish sauce, or turn it into an Indian- or Italian-style supper

Serves 4
Prep 10 mins **Total time** 50 mins

500g new potatoes, thinly sliced
1 red onion, cut into wedges
100g radishes, quartered
2 tbsp olive oil
250g cooked beetroot, cut into wedges
4 skinless salmon fillets
a handful of pea shoots
2 tbsp chopped dill
1 tbsp capers

1 Preheat the oven to 200°C, fan 180°C, gas 6. Tip the potatoes into a large, shallow roasting tin and add the red onion and radishes. Drizzle with the oil and add some seasoning. Toss everything together and spread out in the tin. Scatter with the beetroot wedges. Roast for 30 minutes.

2 Remove the tin from the oven and give everything a stir. Put the salmon on top of the vegetables, season and roast for 10-12 minutes until the salmon is just cooked and the vegetables are tender.

3 Transfer the salmon to a plate. Stir the pea shoots into the vegetables, then return the salmon to the tin and scatter over the dill and capers to serve.
■ 454cals; 23g fat (4g sat fat); 34.8g protein; 4.6g fibre; 29g carbs; 8g total sugars; 0.7g salt

ALSO TRY
Indian-style salmon

Preheat the oven to 200°C, fan 180°C, gas 6. Tip 4 medium **sweet potatoes**, peeled and cut into chunks, into a large, shallow roasting tin, add the 1 **red onion**, cut into wedges, 250g halved **cherry tomatoes**, 1 tablespoon **medium curry powder**; and drizzle over 2 tablespoons **olive oil**. Season and toss everything together then spread out in the tin. Roast for 30 minutes. Stir in 1 x 410g tin **chickpeas**, drained and rinsed, and top with 4 skinless **salmon fillets**. Season and roast for 10-12 minutes until the salmon is just cooked and the vegetables are tender. Remove the salmon, stir in a large handful of **young-leaf spinach** and return the salmon to the tin. Scatter over 2 tablespoons chopped **coriander** to serve. **Serves 4.**
■ 595cals; 25g fat (4g sat fat); 38.7g protein; 12.6g fibre; 57g carbs; 14g total sugars; 0.9g salt

Italian-style salmon

Preheat the oven to 200°C, fan 180°C, gas 6. Tip 1 x 500g pack fresh **potato gnocchi** into a large, shallow roasting tin, add 1 **red onion**, cut into wedges, 2 **courgettes**, trimmed and sliced on the diagonal, a handful of **mixed olives**, 1 **lemon**, cut into wedges and drizzle over 2 tablespoons **olive oil**. Season and toss everything together. Spread out in the tin and roast for 30 minutes. Give everything a stir and put 4 **skinless salmon fillets** on top of the vegetables. Season and roast for another 10-12 minutes until the salmon is just cooked and the vegetables are tender. Remove the salmon to a plate. Stir a handful of **rocket** into the vegetables, then return the salmon to the tin and scatter over 2 tbsp chopped **flat-leaf parsley** to serve. **Serves 4.**
■ 547cals; 25g fat (4g sat fat); 36.5g protein; 4.3g fibre; 45g carbs; 3g total sugars; 1.7g salt

KITCHEN *Secret*

To check if salmon is cooked, gently peek using the tip of a small sharp knife – the fish should be opaque.

Smoky fish bake

Rachel Khoo cooked this recipe for her friends for an exclusive magazine photo shoot – it is simplicity itself and really tasty. Serve with a leafy salad

Serves 6

Prep 30 mins **Total time** 1 hr 10 mins
Get ahead Assemble to the end of step 5 up to 2 hrs ahead; chill but bring back to room temperature before baking

- 1.5kg potatoes, cooked and peeled
- 400g skinless and boneless smoked haddock fillet
- 2 handfuls of chopped parsley
- 2 handfuls of grated mature cheese, such as Gruyère, Comté or mature cheddar

For the béchamel sauce

- 50g butter
- 50g plain flour
- 1 litre lukewarm milk, plus extra to thin the sauce if needed
- ½ onion, skin removed
- 2 cloves
- 2 bay leaves
- a generous pinch of ground nutmeg

1 To make the béchamel, melt the butter in a pan over a medium heat. Add the flour and beat hard until you have a smooth paste. Take off the heat, leave to cool for 2 minutes, then gradually add the milk, whisking constantly.

2 Return the pan to a medium heat; add the onion, cloves and bay leaf and simmer for 10 minutes, whisking frequently. If the sauce becomes too thick, whisk in a little more milk.

3 Finish the sauce by removing the onion, clove and bay leaves, then add the nutmeg and season with salt and white pepper. Leave to cool slightly.

4 Preheat the oven to 180°C, fan 160°C, gas 4. Slice the potatoes into 1cm-thick rounds. Cut the haddock into small chunks and add to the béchamel sauce with most of the parsley. Mix together, then add the potatoes.

5 Transfer to a 22 x 28cm (2.5 litre capacity) baking dish and top with the grated cheese.

6 Bake for 35 minutes, or until bubbling. Sprinkle with the reserved chopped parsley before serving.

- 383cals; 15g fat (9g sat fat); 21g protein; 4g fibre; 40g carbs; 7g total sugars; 1.4g salt

KITCHEN *Secret*

The bake also works well with smoked cod fillet, instead of the haddock.

THE LITTLE PARIS KITCHEN BY RACHEL KHOO (MICHAEL JOSEPH, 2012) © 2012 BY RACHEL KHOO

Snacks
and Sides

Recipes

Beef sliders with red onion pickle

Sliders are mini burgers – our version was very popular at our *Sainsbury's magazine* party for the great and the good of the foodie world

Makes 8

Prep 30 mins **Total time** 45 mins
Get ahead Make the burgers, pickle and watercress crème fraîche a few hours ahead; chill. Cook and assemble the burgers just before serving. The uncooked burgers can be frozen

> **250g beef mince**
> **1 shallot, finely diced**
> **1 tsp Worcestershire sauce**
> **1 large egg, plus 1 large egg yolk**
> **100g cheddar, grated**
> **1 tsp caster sugar**
> **8 mini white snack rolls**
> **1 tsp poppy or sesame seeds**
> **olive oil, for frying**
> *For the red onion pickle*
> **½ small red onion, finely sliced**
> **1 tbsp cider vinegar**
> **1 tsp caster sugar**
> *For the watercress crème fraîche*
> **a small handful of watercress, leaves picked, stalks discarded**
> **4 tbsp crème fraîche**
> **a squeeze of lemon juice**

1 For the red onion pickle, toss the onion with the vinegar, sugar and a generous pinch each of salt and pepper. Leave for at least 30 minutes.

2 Preheat the oven to 200°C, fan 180°C, gas 6. Combine the minced beef, shallot, Worcestershire sauce, egg yolk and half the cheddar in a bowl and season with ¼ teaspoon each of sea salt and freshly ground black pepper. Divide the mixture into 8 and shape into patties.

3 To make the watercress crème fraîche, finely chop the watercress leaves, stir into the crème fraîche with the lemon juice and season.

4 Whisk the remaining egg with the sugar and a generous pinch of salt until the sugar has dissolved. Brush over the mini rolls and sprinkle over the poppy or sesame seeds. Put the rolls on a baking sheet and bake for 5 minutes until the tops are brown and glossy. Remove from the oven, slice open and keep warm under a clean tea towel.

5 Preheat the grill to high. Fry the burgers in a little oil in a nonstick frying pan for 5 minutes, turning once, until browned all over and cooked through. Top each burger with a small mound of the remaining cheese, place on a baking tray and grill for 3-4 minutes until melted and bubbling. Serve in the buns, topped with a few slices of the red onion pickle and a spoonful of watercress crème fraîche.

■ 277cals; 18g fat (8g sat fat); 14g protein; 1g fibre; 16g carbs; 3g total sugars; 0.8g salt

ON THE SIDE
Zingy slaw

Whisk the juice of ½ **lemon** with 3 tablespoons of **olive oil**, some seasoning and a pinch of **sugar** in a large bowl. Finely shred 1 bulb of **fennel**, halved and cored, 1 crisp **red apple**, cored, and ¼ **red cabbage**, cored, either by hand or in a food processor, adding each ingredient to the dressing as you shred it. Mix everything together so it's all well coated with the dressing (this will stop the apple discolouring). Scatter over **snipped cress** to serve. **Serves 4**.

■ 114cals; 9g fat (1g sat fat); 1.2g protein; 3.5g fibre; 9g carbs; 8g total sugars; 0g salt

Smoked haddock and cheese jacket potatoes

You can't beat a jacket potato for a simple lunch or supper. Liven them up with one of *Tamsin Burnett-Hall*'s tasty fillings

Serves 4
Prep 1 hr 30 mins
Total time 1 hr 45 mins

4 baking potatoes, around 300g each
a little vegetable oil
300g skinless and boneless smoked haddock fillet
100ml milk
75g cheddar, grated
2 spring onions, trimmed and finely chopped (optional)

1 Preheat the oven to 200°C, fan 180°C, gas 6. Prick the potatoes lightly with a fork. Rub with a little vegetable oil and bake in the oven for 1 hour 15 minutes or until the skins are really crisp and the potatoes are cooked inside.

2 About 15 minutes before the potatoes are ready, place the smoked haddock in a small roasting tin with the milk. Cover with foil and cook in the oven for 8 minutes, then flake the fish into pieces, reserving the cooking milk.

3 Cut the potatoes in half and scoop the insides into a bowl. Mash with enough of the cooking milk to give a soft fluffy texture. Season, then stir in the flaked smoked haddock.

4 Pile back into the potato shells, place on a baking tray and scatter over the cheese and spring onions (if using). Return to the oven for 15 minutes until the cheese is golden brown.
■ 404cals; 11g fat (5g sat fat); 26g protein; 4g fibre; 53g carbs; 3.5g total sugars; 0.5g salt

ALSO TRY
Cheat's chilli and guacamole
Soften 1 chopped **onion** in oil, add 250g **beef mince** and brown. Stir in 1 teaspoon **ground cumin** and a good pinch of **chilli powder**. Add 1 x 420g tin **kidney beans in chilli sauce** and 1 x 400g tin **chopped tomatoes**. Simmer for about 30 minutes, stirring now and again; season. Spoon onto the halved baked potatoes. Top with **guacamole** and/or **soured cream** and **chopped coriander**. **Serves 4**.
■ 472cals; 13.8g fat (4.9g sat fat); 23.7g protein; 10.4g fibre; 62.6g carbs; 9.1g total sugars; 0.84g salt

Three cheese and onion
Mix 75g each of **coarsely grated mature cheddar** and **parmesan**, stir in 75g chopped **goats' cheese** and 4 finely chopped **spring onions**; season. Divide between the cooked and halved baked potatoes, put them on a baking sheet and put back in the oven for 5 minutes to melt the cheeses before serving. **Serves 4**.
■ 444cals; 17.6g fat (11g sat fat); 21.6g protein; 5.4g fibre; 49.4g carbs; 2.6g total sugars; 1g salt

Hot-smoked mackerel fillets are also delicious in this recipe – just omit step 2.

'MAKE THIS AND EAT IT *straightaway* TO ENJOY THE FRESH FLAVOURS'

KITCHEN Secret

Try this as a salad instead – replace the baguette with a few handfuls of cooked rice noodles.

Warm Vietnamese pork baguette

Warm, sticky pork, crunchy vegetables and fiery chilli – this recipe by *Sarah Randell* is a twist on the classic Vietnamese sandwich, *banh mi*

Serves 4
Prep 20 mins, plus marinating
Total time 35 mins
Get ahead Marinate the pork
a few hours ahead

500g pork tenderloin fillet
1 garlic clove, crushed
1 tbsp Thai fish sauce
3 tbsp light soy sauce
3 tbsp rice wine vinegar
1 tsp caster sugar
1 small carrot, sliced into
thin batons
3 radishes, sliced
¼ white cabbage, core removed,
finely shredded
2 spring onions, trimmed
and sliced
1 red chilli, sliced (deseed the chilli
if you don't like things too hot)
a handful of mixed coriander
and mint leaves
1 stonebaked baguette
2 tbsp mayonnaise

1 Trim and slice the pork into 1cm-thick discs. In a bowl, mix the garlic, fish sauce and soy sauce. Add the pork discs, turn in the marinade and set aside. Preheat a griddle pan.

2 In a second bowl, mix the vinegar and sugar with a pinch of salt. Toss in the carrot, radishes and shredded cabbage. In a third small bowl, mix the spring onions, chilli and herbs.

3 Griddle the discs of pork in batches for 2-3 minutes on each side until browned and cooked through, brushing them with any leftover marinade as they cook.

4 Halve the baguette lengthways and spread the inside with the mayonnaise. Pile in the pickled carrot, radish and cabbage, top with the pork and scatter the spring onion mixture on top of that. Slice into four and devour.

■ 510cals; 13g fat (3g sat fat); 38g protein; 5.3g fibre; 64g carbs; 10g total sugars; 4.6g salt

ALSO TRY
Ruth Watson's smoked salmon, horseradish, pancetta and watercress bagels
Preheat the grill to its highest setting. Grill 2 x 70g packs **sliced pancetta**, or the same quantity of rindless bacon, on a large nonstick baking tray for a few minutes, until crisp; drain on kitchen paper. Slice 4 **plain bagels** in half horizontally and lightly toast the cut sides. Mix 4 tablespoons **crème fraîche** and 2 teaspoons strong **creamed horseradish** together in a small bowl. To make each bagel, spread a slice of **smoked salmon** with a little horseradish cream and put it on the bagel. Top with some pancetta or bacon and, finally, a few sprigs of **watercress**. Spread the other half of the bagel with a little more horseradish cream and press together. **Serves 4.**

■ 450cals; 21.7g fat (8.5g sat fat); 24.6g protein; 0.3g fibre; 38.6g carbs; 5.2g total sugars; 3.7g salt

Spanish-style bubble and squeak

Sam and *Sam Clark*'s restaurant, Moro, is one of our favourites.
Try their bubble and squeak recipe on its own or with sausages

Serves 4-6
Prep 15 mins **Total time** 55 mins

**500g potatoes, peeled and
cut into chunks**
6 tbsp olive oil
3 garlic cloves, peeled and sliced
**12 rashers smoked pancetta, 8 left
whole, the rest chopped**
**500g medium turnips, peeled and
cut into 1cm dice**
**300g spring greens, trimmed and
cut into bite-sized pieces**
1 tsp fresh thyme leaves
2 pinches grated nutmeg (optional)

1 Cook the potatoes in boiling salted
water until tender, then drain.
Meanwhile, in a large frying pan,
heat 2 tablespoons of the oil over
a medium heat. Add the garlic and
chopped pancetta and fry for a couple
of minutes until they begin to colour.
Stir in the turnips, cook for 5 minutes
until beginning to soften, then add the
greens. Season and add the thyme
and the nutmeg, if using.

2 Continue to cook for 20 minutes, stirring

regularly. Remove from the heat and tip
into a bowl. Roughly mash the potatoes.
Stir them into the mixture, mash a little
more and season.

3 Wipe out the frying pan and heat
another 2 tablespoons of the oil over
a high heat. When hot, tip the mixture
into the pan and press down firmly
with a spoon until the base of the pan
is covered. Give it a shake, reduce the
heat to medium and cook for 5-10
minutes or until brown underneath.

4 Turn the bubble and squeak over; to do
this place a plate on top of the pan and
invert the bubble and squeak onto it.
Put the remaining oil in the pan, briefly
increase the heat until it smokes, then
slide the bubble and squeak off the
plate and back into the pan.

5 Again, reduce the heat to medium
and fry for 5 minutes. Meanwhile, fry
or grill the pancetta rashers for a few
minutes until crisp. Serve warm on top
of the bubble and squeak.

■ 287cals; 17.8g fat, (4.5g sat fat);
13g protein; 4.9g fibre; 20g carbs;
20g total sugars; 2.2g salt

KITCHEN
Secret

For a spicy twist, use thin
slices of crisped chorizo
instead of the rashers of
smoked pancetta.

Anna Del Conte

Anna is an Italian legend and has written for the magazine since the early days. These are two of her favourite side dishes that she cooks at home

Anna was first featured in *Sainsbury's magazine* in October 1993. She began writing about Italian food in the 1960s, introducing us Brits to regional recipes, in particular specialities from northern Italy. Anna's books are a great introduction for anyone who wants to learn how to cook Italian – she is a stickler for authenticity and passionate about great food.

Peperonata

Serves 6-8
Prep 25 mins **Total time** 1 hr 5 mins

1.5kg mixed red, yellow
and green peppers
400g large mild onions,
finely sliced
100ml extra-virgin olive oil
3 garlic cloves, peeled and sliced
700g ripe tomatoes, peeled,
deseeded and chopped
4 tbsp chopped fresh
flat-leaf parsley

1 Quarter and deseed the mixed
peppers, then cut each quarter
lengthways into 1cm strips.
2 Fry the onions in the oil in a deep-
sided frying pan over a medium heat
until soft, stirring frequently. Add the
garlic, peppers and a pinch of salt
and cook for a further 10 minutes,
mixing every now and then.
3 Stir in the tomatoes, bring to a
simmer, then turn the heat down and
let the whole thing cook for about 25
minutes, stirring occasionally. Do not
cover the pan, so the tomato juices
can thicken. Add pepper to taste and
sprinkle with the parsley. Add a splash
of red wine vinegar, if you like. Cook
for a further 1-2 minutes then transfer
to a serving bowl. Serve hot or cold,
but never chilled.

■ 175cals; 10.2g fat, (1.6g sat fat);
3.1g protein; 6.1g fibre; 17.4g carbs;
16.1g total sugars; 0g salt

ALSO TRY
Cannellini beans
with sage and garlic

Soak 350g dried **cannellini** beans
overnight. Drain, then put them into
a large pan and cover with fresh cold
water. Add 1 small **onion** and 2 **sage
leaves** and bring to the boil. Boil for
10 minutes, uncovered, then remove
the scum, reduce the heat, cover and
simmer for a further 1¼-1½ hours or
until tender. Drain and discard the onion
and sage leaves. Put 6 tablespoons of
extra-virgin olive oil in a large frying
pan with 2 sprigs of **fresh sage** and
4 chopped **garlic cloves**. Cook until
the sage begins to sizzle and the garlic
smells aromatic. Stir for a minute, then
mix in the beans and stir until they are
covered in the oil. Pour in 120ml
vegetable stock and season. Simmer,
uncovered, for a couple of minutes until
the stock has been absorbed. Remove
and discard the sage, or leave it in and
eat it, if you prefer. **Serves 8**.

■ 197cals; 8.5g fat, (1.2g sat fat);
8.9g protein; 5g fibre; 22.8g carbs;
2g total sugars; 0.3g salt

Peas à la Française

It sounds French, but **Ruth Watson**'s recipe couldn't be more English – use all that's best from the summer vegetable patch

Serves 4-6
Prep 15 **Total time** 35 mins

110g baby carrots
1 Little Gem lettuce
8 spring onions
150ml vegetable stock or water
450g shelled peas
1 tsp sugar
75g butter
1 tbsp chopped tarragon
2 tbsp chopped flat-leaf parsley

1 Chop the carrots on the diagonal – to do this, place the carrot flat on a board (west to east) and, starting about 2.5cm from the thin end, slice through on a diagonal, starting at the 10 o'clock position and finishing at 4 o'clock. Roll the carrot approximately a quarter turn towards you and repeat the cut. Carry on turning and slicing until you reach the end.

2 Cut the lettuce into 1cm slices and pull roughly apart so you have a shredded mass. Trim the spring onions and slice into 2.5cm chunks.

3 Put the carrots in a pan with the water or stock, bring to the boil and, with the lid on, simmer for 6-7 minutes, until they are half-cooked. Add the peas, spring onions, lettuce, sugar, 50g of the butter and a little salt. Bring back to the boil and simmer, uncovered, gently for another 8-10 minutes, stirring often.

4 When the carrots are cooked and the lettuce and spring onions have wilted, remove the pan from the heat and stir in the herbs and the rest of the butter. Taste to see if more salt is needed and give the dish a generous grinding of black pepper.

■ 171cals; 11.5g fat (7g sat fat); 5.6g protein; 5.8g fibre; 11.3g carbs; 5g total sugars; 0.2g salt

KITCHEN
Secret

In the winter months, use frozen peas; just defrost them first and give them 5 minutes less cooking time.

Baked tomatoes with mozzarella and anchovies

Anchovies, basil and mozzarella transform ordinary tomatoes into a tempting Italian-style side. Recipe by *Sarah Randell*

Serves 2
Prep 10 mins **Total time** 30 mins

4 tomatoes, halved
olive oil
4 anchovies, drained and
finely chopped
3 tbsp breadcrumbs
a small handful of shredded basil,
plus extra to finish
1 ball of mozzarella, drained
and chopped

1 Preheat the oven to 200°C, fan 180°C, gas 6. Arrange the tomatoes, cut-side up, in a shallow baking dish. Drizzle with a little olive oil, season and scatter over the chopped anchovies. Bake for 10 minutes.

2 Meanwhile, mix the breadcrumbs with a small handful of shredded basil. Remove the tomatoes from the oven, scatter with the mozzarella, followed by the basil and breadcrumb mixture. Bake for a further 8-10 minutes. Sprinkle with extra shredded basil to serve.

■ 295cals; 15g fat (9g sat fat); 17g protein; 3.3g fibre; 22g carbs; 6.5g total sugars; 1.7g salt

ALSO TRY
Warm lemon, tomato and bean salad
Bring a pan of salted water to the boil. Meanwhile, remove the skin and pith from 1 **lemon**, then dice the flesh. Boil 225g trimmed **fine green beans** for 3-4 minutes or until tender. Halve 250g **cherry tomatoes**, tip them into a bowl with the diced lemon, 3 tablespoons roughly chopped **flat-leaf parsley**, 1 tablespoon small **capers**, drained, and 2 tablespoons **olive oil**. Drain the beans and, while they are still hot, tip them into the bowl and toss with the other ingredients and some seasoning.
Serves 4.
■ 75cals; 6g fat (1g sat fat); 1.6g protein; 2.6g fibre; 3.6g carbs; 3g total sugars; 0g salt

KITCHEN
Secret

If you're not a fan of anchovies, use a little diced smoked bacon or crushed garlic instead.

Lightly spiced potato salad

This salad was from an Indian summer feature that *Anjum Anand* wrote for a September issue of the magazine. Serve with barbecued meats or fish

Serves 6
Prep 15 mins **Total time** 35 mins
Get ahead Make a few hours ahead

750g baby new potatoes
2 tsp vegetable oil
¾ tsp nigella or mustard seeds
½ tsp each cumin and fennel seeds
2 spring onions, trimmed
and finely sliced
5 radishes, trimmed and
finely sliced
For the dressing
6 tbsp olive oil
5 tbsp lemon juice
2 garlic cloves, crushed
into a paste
100ml good-quality mayonnaise

1 Bring the potatoes to the boil in a large pan of salted water. Simmer for 15-20 minutes or until tender.

2 Meanwhile, make the dressing. In a bowl, whisk together the olive oil, lemon juice, garlic paste and mayonnaise. Season to taste.

3 Heat the vegetable oil in a small pan, tilting it so the oil collects in one area. Add the seeds and, when they start to pop, remove from the heat. Leave for 10 seconds, then pour it all into the dressing. Whisk well.

4 Drain the cooked potatoes and, if you like, when cool enough to handle, peel them. Halve or quarter, depending on their size.

5 Tip the potatoes into the dressing, along with the spring onions and radishes and mix well. The potatoes will absorb the dressing as they cool. Season to taste.

■ 314cals; 25g fat (4g sat fat); 2.4g protein; 1.8g fibre; 21g carbs; 2.3g total sugars; 0.2g salt

ALSO TRY
Anjum's mushroom salad

Mix together 4 **garlic cloves**, crushed, a 25g piece of **root ginger**, peeled and finely grated, ¾ teaspoon of **hot or mild chilli powder**, 1 heaped teaspoon of **garam masala**, 1 teaspoon of **ground cumin**, 3½ tablespoons of **lemon juice**, 7 tablespoons of **olive oil** with about 1 teaspoon of salt. Halve or slice 400g **mixed mushrooms**. Toss in the marinade, making sure each piece is coated; leave for 30 minutes. Meanwhile, preheat the grill and whisk together 1½ tablespoons of **cider vinegar**, sherry or white wine vinegar, 4 tablespoons of **olive oil**, ¾ teaspoon of **Dijon mustard** and season. Grill the mushrooms for 3-4 minutes each side or until lightly charred. Layer in a serving bowl with **mixed baby salad leaves**. Drizzle over the dressing and toss well to coat. Sprinkle with chopped **pistachios**, and finely chopped **shallots** to finish **Serves 4**.

■ 329cals; 33.7g fat (4.8g sat fat); 3.5g protein; 2g fibre; 1.7g carbs; 1.3g total sugars; 1g salt

Leek, butternut and sage gratin

A vegetable dish that goes well with roast meats, or serve as a vegetarian main course. Recipe by *Brian Glover*

Serves 4-6
Prep 15 minutes
Total time 1 hour 25 minutes
Get ahead The gratin can be assembled to the end of step 2 the night before; cover and chill. The crumbs can be prepared 2 days in advance; cool and store in an airtight container

1kg butternut squash, peeled, halved and deseeded
25g butter
2 tbsp olive oil
3 large leeks, trimmed and thickly sliced
2 tsp coarsely chopped fresh sage leaves, plus 8-10 small whole leaves
1 x 300ml carton double cream
2 slices of day-old white bread, crusts removed, made into coarse crumbs

1 Cut the squash into 2cm-thick slices. Heat half the butter and half the oil in a large frying pan over a medium heat, add the squash and cook for 5 minutes. Add the leeks and turn the vegetables in the juices. Cook for a few minutes more, then add a pinch of salt, cover and cook for 5 minutes. Uncover, turn up the heat a little and cook, turning the vegetables, until they are tender and starting to brown. Take off the heat, stir in the chopped sage and season. Allow to cool.

2 Preheat the oven to 200°C, fan 180°C, gas 6. Arrange the vegetables in a 1.2 litre ovenproof dish that has been lightly buttered. Stir 2 tablespoons of cold water into the cream, then spoon over the vegetables.

3 Heat the remaining butter and oil in the cleaned frying pan, add the breadcrumbs and fry until golden. Stir in the whole sage leaves and season.

4 Bake the gratin for 35-40 minutes. Scatter over the sage crumbs, then cook for a further 10-15 minutes until browned and bubbling. Let it stand for 5 minutes before serving.

■ 419cals; 35g fat, (19.6g sat fat); 4.7g protein; 4.2g fibre; 23g carbs; 9.8 total sugars; 0.3g salt

ALSO TRY
Sweet potato and celeriac mash
Preheat the oven to 190°C, fan 170°C, gas 5. Bake 4 **sweet potatoes** (about 500g) in their skins for 50-60 minutes until soft, cool a little, then peel and place the flesh in a food processor. While the potatoes are cooking, peel 700g **celeriac** and cut it into chunks, then cook in boiling salted water with 2 **garlic cloves** (unpeeled) for 15-20 minutes or until tender. Drain well and add to the food processor, popping the garlic out of its skin. Add 25g **butter**, 4 tbsp **crème fraîche** and 1 tbsp **olive oil**, then whiz to a purée. Transfer to a pan, taste and add some seasoning and a grating of **nutmeg**. Serve hot topped with a knob of **butter** and some **black pepper. Serves 4**.
■ 287cals; 17g fat, (9.1g sat fat); 4g protein; 12.6g fibre; 28.9g carbs; 10.1g total sugars; 0.67g salt

KITCHEN *Secret*

Make the gratin to accompany roast beef – use thyme instead of the sage.

Rachel Allen

With just a few extra ingredients, Rachel's recipes for simple side dishes turn run-of-the-mill vegetables into something really special

The Ballymaloe Cookery School is held in great reverence at *Sainsbury's magazine* – the school has trained many well-known chefs (see the sweet white scones on page 169 by Darina Allen, the founder of the school). Rachel Allen also teaches there and is a well-known figure on our television screens and a busy, bestselling author. She lives by the sea in Country Cork with her family.

Ribboned carrots with honey and parsley

Use a flat-sided peeler to slice 1kg **carrots** into long ribbons. Fill a large pan with water, add 1 teaspoon of **salt**, bring to the boil and blanch the carrots for 30 seconds. Drain. Place a small pan over a medium heat, add 50g **butter** and 2 tablespoons **clear honey** and, as the butter melts, stir to combine. Drizzle over the carrots, add 6 tablespoons chopped **flat-leaf parsley**, toss to combine. Season to taste, then serve. **Serves 8**.

■ 105cals; 6g fat (3g sat fat); 0.7g protein; 3g fibre; 14g carbs; 13g total sugars; 0.2g salt

Green beans with lemon and pine nuts

Cook 600g **fine green beans** in a pan of boiling salted water for 3–4 minutes, drain. Put another large pan over a medium heat, add 4 tablespoons **olive oil**, 100g **pine nuts** and 4 **garlic cloves**, finely sliced, and cook for 2 minutes, until golden. Add the beans and the zest and juice of 1 large **lemon**. Season and serve. **Serves 8**.

■ 153cals; 14.4g fat (1.4g sat fat); 3.2g protein; 2.5g fibre; 2.7g carbs; 2.1g total sugars; 0g salt

Southern cornbread

A classic from American baking specialists *David Lesniak* and *David Muniz*. Plus, our favourite tear-and-share bread recipe

Serves 12
Prep 10 mins
Total time 1 hr 10 mins
Get ahead Make up to 2 days ahead

125g unsalted butter, melted,
plus extra for greasing
350g plain flour
175g polenta
150g granulated sugar
4 tsp baking powder
500ml double cream
2 large eggs
1 x 198g tin sweetcorn, drained,
or use the equivalent weight of
fresh or frozen

1 Preheat the oven to 200°C, fan 180°C, gas 6. Grease a 5cm-deep, 20cm-square baking tin with melted butter. In a medium sized bowl, combine the flour, polenta, sugar, baking powder and 1 teaspoon of salt. Set aside.

2 In the bowl of an electric food mixer or with an electric hand whisk, combine the melted butter, double cream and eggs. On a slow speed, gradually add the dry ingredients until everything is combined and no lumps remain. Stir the sweetcorn into the batter.

3 Pour the mixture into the prepared tin and bake for 1 hour until lightly golden and springy to the touch. Cut into 12 squares and serve.

■ 520cals; 33g fat (20g sat fat); 7g protein; 2g fibre; 47g carbs; 14g total sugars; 0.3g salt;

ALSO TRY
Blue cheese, red onion and pancetta bread

Tip 1 x 500g pack **ciabatta bread mix** into a large bowl. Add 350ml lukewarm water and 1 tablespoon of **olive oil**. Mix together, then knead on a floured surface for a few minutes. Stretch into a 10 x 15cm rectangle, set aside for 15 minutes. Crumble over 65g blue **goats' cheese**. Fold the dough and knead

briefly to incorporate the cheese. Transfer to a large, lightly floured baking tray and stretch into a 20 x 28cm rectangle. Leave to rise in a warm place for 20 minutes. Preheat the oven to 230°C, fan 210°C, gas 8. Fry 75g cubed **pancetta** until browned, scoop into a small bowl. Add 1 tablespoon of **oil**, 1 large, finely sliced **red onion** and 1 teaspoon **sugar** to the pan and fry for 10 minutes; add to the pancetta. Use your thumbs to make a few indentations in the top of the dough, and poke in small sprigs of **rosemary**. Scatter with rosemary needles, 65g crumbled blue **goats' cheese** and the pancetta and onions. Sprinkle with **sea salt** and a drizzle of oil. Bake for 15-20 minutes until golden. Reduce the temperature to 180°C, fan 160°C, gas 4 and cook for 10 minutes more. Eat warm or cold. **Serves 6-8**.

■ 339cals; 12g fat (5g sat fat); 11g protein; 3g fibre; 51g carbs; 2g total sugars; 0.6g salt

Desserts and Puddings

Recipes

Nigella Lawson

This is a failsafe stand-by dessert recipe. Mascarpone has a longish fridge life, so you can keep all the ingredients to hand and make it in no time

The original Domestic Goddess, Nigella Lawson is an award-winning cookbook author and TV chef whose relaxed way with food has captivated hearts across the world. Michael Wynn-Jones – Delia's husband and the editor of the magazine in the 1990s – asked Nigella to contribute. This is one of the first Nigella recipes we published.

Mascarpone, rum and lime creams

Serves 4
Prep 15 mins **Total time** 15 mins, plus cooling
Get ahead Make and chill a few hours ahead

- 3 large eggs, separated
- 100g caster sugar
- 350g mascarpone
- 3 tbsp dark rum
- juice and zest of 1-2 limes

1 Whisk the egg yolks and sugar together until light and creamy. In another bowl, combine the mascarpone with the rum and the juice of 1 lime. Gently fold the egg mixture into the mascarpone. Taste it and add a little more lime juice if needed. What you want is the creamy tartness of cheesecake with the lightness of a mousse.

2 Wipe the inside of a clean bowl with the cut side of one of the squeezed limes, add the egg whites and whisk them with clean beaters until stiff. Carefully fold them into the mascarpone mixture, then divide the finished cream between 4 x 225-250ml serving glasses, decorate with lime zest and chill until needed.

Note: this recipe contains raw/partially cooked eggs.

- 570cals; 44.1g fat (27.1g sat fat); 9.8g protein; 0g fibre; 27.9g carbs; 27.9g total sugars; 0.28g salt

Pavlova with nectarines, redcurrants and elderflower syllabub

Change the fruit to suit the seasons – apricots, plums or gooseberries would all work well. Recipe by *Sarah Randell*

Serves 8
Prep 20 mins **Total time** 1 hr 20 mins, plus cooling
Get ahead Bake the meringue the day before

    4 large egg whites
    225g caster sugar (unrefined gives the meringue a nice colour)
    1 tsp cornflour
    1 tsp white wine vinegar
For the syllabub
    300ml whipping cream
    2 tbsp caster sugar
    3 tbsp elderflower cordial
    zest of 1 lemon and 1 tbsp lemon juice
    4 nectarines or 8 apricots
    a handful of redcurrants, on the stalk

1. Preheat the oven to 140°C, fan 120°C, gas 1. In a large, clean bowl, whisk the egg whites until they form stiff peaks. Add the sugar, a spoonful at a time, whisking continuously. Add the cornflour and vinegar with the last spoonful.
2. Pile the meringue onto a baking tray lined with baking paper to form a circle roughly 22cm in diameter, making swirls and peaks.
3. Bake the meringue for 1 hour, turn the oven off and leave the meringue inside until completely cold.
4. For the syllabub, whip the cream and the sugar until it forms soft peaks. Stir in the elderflower cordial and the lemon zest and juice. Halve, de-stone and slice the nectarines or apricots; toss with the redcurrants. Top the pavlova with the syllabub and fruit.

■ 300cals; 15g fat (10g sat fat); 3.2g protein; 1.2g fibre; 41g carbs; 41g total sugars; 0.1g salt

ALSO TRY
Mark Hix's iced berries with hot white chocolate sauce
Place 225g **white chocolate buttons or grated white chocolate** and 300ml **double cream** in a heatproof bowl over a pan of simmering water for 20-30 minutes, stirring every so often. When the sauce is hot you're ready to go. Divide 500g **frozen berries** between 4 dessert plates and leave at room temperature for 10-15 minutes, to lose a little of their chill. Transfer the hot sauce to a jug and pour it over the frozen berries at the table.
Serves 4.

■ 650cals; 51g fat, (31g sat fat); 7g protein; 1.5g fibre; 42g carbs; 39g total sugars; 0.2g salt

KITCHEN *Secret*

Adding vinegar to the meringue mixture helps stabilise the egg white to make a crisp meringue with a gooey middle.

Chocolate orange cheesecake

Chocolate and orange are made for each other – this baked cheesecake by *Brian Glover* has just the right balance of sweetness and citrussy zing

Serves 10-12

Prep 30 mins **Total time** 1 hr 20 mins, plus cooling and chilling overnight
Get ahead Make the day before; chill

- 500g full-fat cream cheese
- 150ml soured cream
- 125g caster sugar
- 1 rounded tbsp cornflour
- 2 large eggs, plus 2 egg yolks
- juice and zest of 1 orange
- juice of 1 small lemon
- 1 tsp vanilla extract

For the base
- 150g digestive biscuits
- 75g unsalted butter, melted
- 4 tsp cocoa powder

For the topping
- 100g dark chocolate, broken into pieces
- 150ml soured cream
- 100g caster sugar
- 6 thin slices of clementine

1 Preheat the oven to 180°C, fan 160°C, gas 4. Line the base and sides of a 22-23cm springform cake tin with baking paper, so the paper comes 2.5cm above the tin edge.

2 For the base, crush the biscuits and mix with the melted butter and cocoa powder. Tip into the tin and press down gently; bake for 10 minutes. Remove from the oven, then lower the temperature to 160°C, fan 140°C, gas 3.

3 Beat together the cream cheese and soured cream, then beat in the sugar and cornflour. Separately, beat the eggs, yolks, orange and lemon juice and vanilla. Gradually combine the two mixtures; beat until smooth. Mix in the orange zest.

4 Tip the mixture onto the biscuit base and bake the cheesecake for 40 minutes, then turn the oven off and leave the cheesecake inside to cool.

5 For the topping, melt the dark chocolate and soured cream in a bowl over a pan of barely simmering water; stir until smooth. Cool, then spread over the cooled cheesecake. Cover and chill overnight.

6 In a pan, dissolve the 100g of caster sugar in 3 tablespoons of water over a low heat. Increase the heat, let it bubble for 2-3 minutes to make a syrup, then add the slices of clementine. Bubble for 5-6 minutes until the slices look translucent. Transfer to a baking sheet lined with baking paper to cool. Remove the cheesecake from the tin, decorate with the clementine slices and serve.

■ 498cals; 37g fat (22g sat fat); 6g protein; 1g fibre; 35g carbs; 28g total sugars; 0.6g salt

ALSO TRY
Passionfruit, mango and lime cheesecake

For the base: Omit the cocoa powder and add 1 teaspoon **ground ginger**. For the filling: Use the finely grated zest of 2 **limes** and the juice of 4 **limes** instead of the orange and lemon. Increase the vanilla to 2 teaspoons. For the topping: Warm the pulp of 8-10 **passionfruit** in a pan; strain into a measuring jug. Reserve 2 tablespoons of the pips. Add the juice of 2 **limes**, 3 teaspoons of **caster sugar** and some water, if needed, to make 120ml. Mix 2 tablespoons of the juice with 2 teaspoons of **arrowroot**, then mix this into the jug. Heat the juice gently in a pan, stirring until thick and smooth. Add the reserved pips, cool. Spread 4-5 tablespoons **mascarpone cheese** over the chilled cheesecake, top with 1 sliced **mango** and 1 sliced **papaya**, and some **physalis**. Drizzle with the juice to serve.

■ 431cals; 34g fat (21g sat fat); 5g protein; 2g fibre; 25g carbs; 17g total sugars; 0.6g salt

KITCHEN
Secret

Cooling cheesecakes in a
turned-off oven helps to
minimise cracking on the
top of the filling.

White chocolate mousse brûlées with prunes

Alex Mackay's indulgent brûlées are a treat to share, and prunes and Armagnac are a match made in heaven

Serves 6

Prep time 20 mins **Total time** 30 mins, plus 10 mins' soaking and chilling
Get ahead The mousse will keep, covered, in the fridge for up to 2 days. It can be brûléed 30 minutes before serving, then returned to the fridge, uncovered, until ready to serve

- 12 pitted prunes, quartered
- 2 tablespoons Armagnac or cognac
- 1 vanilla pod
- 150ml double cream
- 250g white chocolate, broken into chunks
- 2 large egg whites
- 6 tbsp demerara sugar

1 Put the prunes in a small bowl with the Armagnac or cognac and soak for at least 10 minutes. Meanwhile, split the vanilla pod in half, scrape out the seeds and add them to the cream in a medium-size bowl. Whip to firm peaks and set aside in the fridge.

2 Melt the chocolate in a bowl over a pan of barely simmering water, then turn off the heat. In a large, clean bowl, whisk the egg whites to firm peaks, then fold into the cream. Check the chocolate – it should be just lukewarm. Briskly stir one-third of the cream mixture into the chocolate, then fold this into the remaining two-thirds of cream mixture to make a mousse.

3 Divide the prunes and any leftover soaking juices between 6 flameproof cups or ramekins. Spoon the mousse over the top, smoothing the tops. Chill to set for at least 3 hours.

4 Cover the top of each mousse with a generous sprinkling of demerara. (Wipe the sides of the cups or ramekins, or the sugar will burn onto the rims.) Caramelise with a cooks' blowtorch, starting from about 10cm away to melt the sugar all over, then moving closer for a golden finish.
Note: this recipe contains raw/ partially cooked eggs.

■ 446cals; 26.4g fat (16g sat fat); 5.3g protein; 1.7g fibre; 45.3g carbs; 45.3g total sugars; 0.2g salt

KITCHEN Secret

If you like, you could just serve the mousse – follow the recipe but leave out the prunes and brûléeing.

Anjum Anand

In this recipe, buttermilk is used instead of cream – it is slightly tangy and goes beautifully with the plums

Anjum Anand is known for her healthy take on Indian food, creating traditional dishes with a contemporary approach. The *Sainsbury's magazine* cookery team are great fans of her first book, *Indian Every Day: Light Healthy Indian Food*. Anjum now has several other titles to her name, has had her own television series and launched a range of Indian sauces – there's no stopping her!

Buttermilk panna cottas with roasted plums

Serves 6
Prep 15 mins **Total time** 45 mins, plus setting

- 4 leaves fine-leaf gelatine
- 250ml double cream
- 100g caster sugar
- zest of 1 orange
- 500ml buttermilk
- 1½ tsp vanilla extract

For the roasted plums
- 6 plums, stoned and cut into wedges
- 45g caster sugar
- 125ml orange juice
- 3 tsp lime juice
- 3 star anise, halved
- 40g butter, cubed

1 Soak the gelatine in cold water. Heat the cream with the sugar and a good teaspoon of the orange zest in a pan over a low heat, stirring until the sugar dissolves. Remove from the heat. Squeeze out the excess water from the gelatine leaves and stir them into the hot cream mixture until dissolved. Stir in the buttermilk and vanilla. Divide between 6 x 175ml pudding basins or ramekins, cover with clingfilm and refrigerate for a few hours or overnight until set.

2 Preheat the oven to 180°C, fan 160°C, gas 4. Fold a large piece of kitchen foil to make a double-thickness square measuring about 30cm. Turn up the edges slightly and put the plums in the middle. Top evenly with the remaining ingredients and pull up the sides of the foil to enclose the plums and flavourings, making sure no juices will leak out. Place on a baking tray and bake for 15-18 minutes or until the plums are tender. Leave to cool until barely warm.

3 Dip the base of the pudding basins or ramekins in boiling water for a few seconds, one at a time, so the panna cottas will slide out easily. Turn onto serving plates, garnish with the remaining orange zest and serve with the plums and juices – if you like, you can put these into a pan and bubble briefly to make them more syrupy.

■ 416cals; 28g fat (18g sat fat); 9.6g protein; 1g fibre; 37g carbs; 37g total sugars; 0.3g salt

Frozen raspberry trifle terrine

This recipe by *Sarah Randell* has all the elements of a traditional boozy trifle, with a contemporary twist

Serves: 8-10
Prep 30 mins **Total time** 35 mins, plus freezing
Get ahead Make up to 2 weeks ahead

> 300g raspberries, plus extra
> to decorate
> 8 tbsp icing sugar
> 300ml double cream
> 1 x 500g tub vanilla custard
> 2 large egg whites
> 4 tbsp Pedro Ximénez or other
> sweet sherry
> 12-16 sponge fingers
> *For the praline*
> 50g granulated or caster sugar
> 40g toasted flaked almonds

1 Line a 22 x 10cm x 7cm-deep loaf tin with clingfilm so it overhangs the edges all the way round. Whiz the 300g of raspberries in a food processor with half of the icing sugar. Strain the purée through a sieve into a bowl, discarding the pips.

2 Whip the cream with the rest of the icing sugar to soft peaks. Fold the custard into the cream and divide between two bowls. Stir the raspberry purée into one bowl.

3 In another clean bowl, whisk the egg whites to soft peaks. Fold half of the egg whites into each custard mixture.

4 Spoon the two mixtures into the prepared loaf tin, alternating spoonfuls of each mixture. Reserve a couple of tablespoons of mixture to use on top of the sponge fingers. Use a skewer to gently swirl the mixtures together.

5 Pour the sherry into a shallow bowl. Dip both sides of the sponge fingers into the sherry and place on top of the mixture in two layers. Finish with a thin layer of the leftover mixture. Cover with the clingfilm and freeze overnight.

6 For the praline, gently melt the sugar in a small pan. When it has turned to a golden caramel, stir in the flaked almonds and tip on to a sheet of baking paper. Leave to set.

7 Transfer the terrine from the freezer to the fridge 30 minutes before serving. Tip it out of the tin, remove the clingfilm and scatter with the praline, broken up, and the extra raspberries. Slice to serve.
Note: this recipe contains raw/ partially cooked eggs.

■ 357cals; 21g fat (12g sat fat); 5g protein; 1g fibre; 37g carbs; 30g total sugars; 0.2g salt

KITCHEN *Secret*

Pedro Ximénez is a thick, sweet Spanish sherry. It's also delicious drizzled over ice cream.

'A TRIFLE YOU CAN SLICE THAT MAKES A GREAT *dinner party* DESSERT'

Layered passionfruit and blackcurrant jellies

Thomasina Miers' Mexican-inspired jellies are an exotic, colourful treat, perfect for a summer's day

Serves 8
Prep 20 mins **Total time** 30 mins, pus chilling and setting overnight
Get ahead Make a couple of days ahead

For the passionfruit jelly
  6 ripe passionfruit
  450-500ml orange juice
  5 leaves fine-leaf gelatine
  150g caster sugar
  a squeeze of lemon juice, if the mixture is too sweet

For the blackcurrant jelly
  4 leaves fine-leaf gelatine
  85g caster sugar
  150g blackcurrants, plus a few extra to decorate
  juice of 1 lime
  1-2 tbsp tequila (optional)

1 First, make the passionfruit jelly. Halve the passionfruit, scoop out the pulp and push it through a sieve, leaving behind only the black seeds (discard these). Tip the juice into a measuring jug and top up with orange juice to make 550ml. Soak the gelatine in cold water until soft. Simmer 150ml water, then stir in the sugar until it dissolves. Squeeze the gelatine to remove any excess water, add it to the simmering syrup and stir to dissolve. Stir in the passionfruit and orange juice, taste and add a squeeze of lemon juice if it's very sweet. Pour into 8 x 250ml glasses and chill for about 4 hours until set before you start the blackcurrant jelly

2 To make the blackcurrant jelly, soak the gelatine leaves in cold water until soft. Dissolve the sugar in 400ml water over a low heat. Add the blackcurrants and simmer for 10 minutes until soft and collapsing. Remove from the heat and push through a sieve, pressing the blackcurrants with the back of a spoon; discard the skins left in the sieve. Return the juice to the pan and place over a low heat. Squeeze the gelatine of excess water and add to the simmering blackcurrant liquid. Stir to dissolve, then strain. Add the lime juice and tequila, if using, and cool.

3 Pour the liquid over the passionfruit jelly and chill overnight until set. Decorate with blackcurrants.

■ 151cals; 0g fat (0g sat fat); 1g protein; 1.5g fibre; 38g carbs; 38g total sugars; 0g salt

KITCHEN *Secret*

Leaf gelatine is preferable to powdered as it will give your jellies a softer set. It's easy to use and keeps well in the storecupboard.

MEXICAN FOOD MADE SIMPLE (HODDER & STOUGHTON, £20)

Rhubarb, rose and white chocolate trifle

A dreamy combination of tart fruit, sweet white chocolate and rich cream, this is the queen of all trifles. Recipe by *Linda Tubby*

Serves: 6-8

Prep time 25 mins **Total time** 55 mins, plus chilling

Get ahead Prepare to the end of step 4 up to a day ahead; chill

> **600g rhubarb, trimmed and cut into 5cm lengths**
> **100ml English Provender Company rose water**
> **175g golden caster sugar**
> **4 leaves fine-leaf gelatine**
> **10 Italian Savoiardi sponge fingers**
> **600ml double cream**
> **2 tbsp icing sugar**
> **100g white chocolate, finely chopped, plus extra for shaving into white chocolate curls**

1 Preheat the oven to 220°C, fan 200°C, gas 7. Spread the rhubarb in a single layer in a large ovenproof dish. Add the rose water and 3 tablespoons of water; scatter over the sugar. Stir, then cover the dish with kitchen foil and bake for 20-25 minutes until soft. Remove from the oven and cool completely.

2 Drain the rhubarb compote through a sieve set over a bowl for 5 minutes, then tip the rhubarb into another bowl. Meanwhile, soak 3 leaves of gelatine in cold water for 5 minutes. Heat 4 tablespoons of the rhubarb juice (there will be about 400ml altogether) in a small pan until bubbling; remove from the heat.

Squeeze the moisture out of the gelatine leaves and add them to the pan. Stir to dissolve, then pour into the bowl with the rest of the juice; mix well. Transfer 75ml of the liquid to a shallow dish, soak the sponge fingers in this, then transfer them to a plate. Pour the rest of the liquid into a trifle dish. Chill for 30-40 minutes until softly set.

3 Arrange the sponge fingers on the set jelly, pressing down lightly. Slowly bring 400ml of the cream to the boil with the icing sugar. Turn the heat down as low as possible and leave for 8 minutes. Meanwhile, soak the remaining gelatine leaf in cold water for 5 minutes. Add the chocolate to the cream, remove from the heat and stir to melt. Squeeze the liquid from the gelatine and stir it into the cream mixture. Transfer to a bowl, then put the bowl in a basin of iced water for 30-40 minutes. Stir now and then until just setting.

4 Pour the cooled cream mixture over the sponge fingers. Chill for 20 minutes or until set, then spoon on the rhubarb and chill until 30 minutes before serving.

5 To serve, softly whip the rest of the cream and spoon it over the trifle. Decorate with white chocolate curls.

■ 598cals; 45g fat (27g sat fat); 4g protein; 2g fibre; 48g carbs; 43g total sugars; 0.1g salt

ALSO TRY
Plum and white chocolate trifle
Replace the rhubarb with 600g **plums**, stoned and cut into wedges. Instead of rosewater, use 100ml freshly squeezed **orange juice**. Bake the plums with the orange juice, water and sugar for 35 minutes. You will only get about 300ml of plum juice (instead of 400ml as with the rhubarb) but the recipe will still work well.

KITCHEN Secret

Use a flat-bladed peeler to make curls from a block of white chocolate.

Apple, blackberry and macadamia nut crumble

Macadamia nuts are an unusual addition to this otherwise traditional recipe by *Fiona Beckett* – they give the crumble a lovely crunchy texture

Serves 6
Prep 30 mins **Total time** 1 hr 10 mins
Get ahead Bake the crumble a few hours ahead and reheat to serve. It freezes well, too

10g butter, plus extra for greasing
3 large Bramley apples
(about 750g)
¼ tsp cinnamon
3-4 tbsp golden caster sugar
375g blackberries
clotted cream or vanilla ice cream, to serve
For the crumble topping
50g macadamia nuts
150g self-raising flour
¼ tsp cinnamon
100g chilled butter, cubed
75g golden caster sugar

1 Lightly grease a medium-sized shallow baking dish with a capacity of 1.5 litres.
2 Peel and core the apples and cut into thick slices. Place in a pan, sprinkle with the cinnamon and 3 tablespoons of the sugar, add the butter and pour over 3 tablespoons of water. Cover the pan, place on a low heat and cook for 8-10 minutes, until the apple slices are soft but still hold their shape. Tip them into the prepared baking dish and set aside to cool.
3 Preheat the oven to 190°C, fan 170°C, gas 5. To make the crumble topping, chop the macadamia nuts roughly in a food processor. Add the flour, cinnamon and butter; pulse until the mixture resembles fine crumbs. Add the sugar and pulse again until the mixture begins to stick together in lumps – you want it to have a coarse consistency.
4 When the apple is cool, gently mix in the blackberries, adding more sugar if they are tart. Spread the crumble mixture evenly over the top and bake on the middle shelf of the oven for about 30 minutes, until the filling is hot and bubbling. Serve with clotted cream or vanilla ice cream.

■ 418cals; 22g fat (10.5g sat fat); 4g protein; 6.7g fibre; 51g carbs; 34.2g total sugars; 0.5g salt

KITCHEN *Secret*

Fancy individual crumbles? Use 6 x 250ml dishes and bake for 20 minutes.

KITCHEN
Secret

For a light pudding,
ensure the creamed
butter, sugar and
eggs are pale before
adding the flour.

Golden pear pudding

An autumnal pudding by *Alex Mackay*. Serve with custard, adding a pinch of ground cinnamon as you warm it through

Serves 6-8

Prep 40 mins **Total time:** 2 hrs 40 mins, plus resting

Get ahead Make the pudding up to a day ahead, cool it in the basin and chill until needed. Steam the pudding gently for 30 minutes to reheat

225g soft unsalted butter, plus extra for greasing
3 large conference pears, peeled, halved and cored
8 tbsp golden syrup
225g caster sugar
2 large eggs and 1 yolk
200g self-raising flour
½ tsp each grated nutmeg and ground cinnamon

1 Heat 25g of the butter in a frying pan until it starts to foam. Fry the pears over a medium heat for 4 minutes on each side until golden. Add 2 tablespoons of golden syrup and simmer for 4 minutes until the sauce begins to caramelise. Leave to cool.

2 In a large bowl, cream the remaining butter with the sugar until pale using an electric hand whisk. Add the eggs and yolk, whisking thoroughly but gently (the mixture needs to be as light as possible) and, finally, whisk in the flour and spices.

3 Pour 3 tablespoons of golden syrup into a 1.5 litre pudding basin that has

been generously buttered, spreading a little of the syrup up the sides. Dip the cut sides of the pears in the syrup and set aside. Put a little of the pudding mixture into the bottom of the basin. Place the pears around the sides of the basin with the cut sides facing outward and their tips facing down.

4 Spoon the rest of the pudding mixture into the centre of the basin, making sure some of the mixture goes in between. Hold the pears against the sides of the basin as you do this so they don't slip too far down.

5 Cover with buttered greaseproof paper, making a pleat in the middle. Tie the paper securely by winding a doubled-up length of string around the rim of the basin. It's a good idea to make a string handle, too (see right).

6 Put the basin into a pan. Fill the pan with boiling water until it comes halfway up the sides of the basin. Cover with a tight-fitting lid and simmer rapidly for 2 hours, topping up the boiling water as needed. Let the pudding rest for 10 minutes then turn it out. Warm the remaining golden syrup in a pan and spoon it over the top.

■ 533cals; 26.2g fat (15.8g sat fat); 4.9g protein; 2.6g fibre; 74.1g carbs; 53g total sugars; 0.4g salt

Make it easy
A string handle will allow you to lift the pudding basin out of the boiling water without the risk of scalding your hands. Just loop a length of string over the top of the basin, under the string that you used to secure the paper cover and back again. Thread it back under the first loop of string and tie in a firm knot. Trim off any excess paper or string before boiling.

Pear, ginger and chocolate cobbler

This fruity, chocolatey, gooey treat by *Sarah Randell* is just perfect for warming you up on a crisp autumnal evening

Serves 4
Prep 15 mins **Total time** 50 mins

5-6 pears, about 1kg in total
a generous pinch of ground ginger
1 tbsp light brown soft sugar
For the topping
50g plain flour
25g ground almonds
3 tbsp demerara sugar, plus
extra for sprinkling
2 tsp baking powder
4 tbsp natural yogurt
50g butter, melted
75-100g dark ginger chocolate
(50% cocoa solids),
roughly chopped
2 tbsp flaked almonds,
for sprinkling
For the Chantilly cream
300ml whipping cream, chilled
1 tbsp icing sugar

1 Preheat the oven to 180°C, fan 160°C, gas 4. For the cobbler topping, mix together the flour, ground almonds, demerara sugar, baking powder and a pinch of salt. Whisk in the yogurt and melted butter.

2 Peel and core the pears, then slice them thickly lengthways. Arrange the slices in a 20-24cm round or square ovenproof dish, toss with the ground ginger, brown sugar and 2 tablespoons of water.

3 Stir the chopped chocolate into the cobbler topping mixture, then dollop it evenly over the pears.

4 Sprinkle with the flaked almonds and extra demerara sugar. Bake for 30-35 minutes or until lightly golden.

5 For the Chantilly cream, whip the cream with the icing sugar and serve with the hot pudding.

■ 785cals; 54.3g fat (29.5g sat fat); 8.3g protein; 8.5g fibre; 65.8g carbs; 57g total sugars; 0.9g salt

ALSO TRY
Easy chocolate mousse
In a pan, bring 125ml **double cream** to the boil. Pour onto 125g **finely chopped dark chocolate** in a bowl and stir to melt. Add 1 tbsp **brandy** (optional) and whisk in 2 large **egg yolks**. In a clean bowl, whisk 2 large **egg whites** to stiff peaks. Stir a small amount into the chocolate mixture, then fold in the rest. Spoon into cups and chill for 1-2 hours until set. Decorate with **raspberries** and dust with **icing sugar**. **Serves 4**.
Note: this recipe contains raw/partially cooked eggs.

■ 391cals; 29.4g fat (16.7g sat fat); 6.6g protein; 1.5g fibre; 23.1g carbs; 23.1g total sugars; 0.1g salt

KITCHEN
Secret

Try this with plums, too – omit the chocolate from the cobbler topping and add the zest of an orange instead.

Recipes

Sweet white scones

Darina Allen is the owner of the highly esteemed Ballymaloe Cookery School in Ireland. Her scone recipe was handed down to her from her mother

Makes 16-18

Prep 30 mins **Total time** 45 mins
Get ahead The scone mixture may be weighed ahead of time – even the day before. The butter may also be rubbed in beforehand, but don't add the baking powder and the liquid until just before baking

**900g plain flour, plus a little
extra for rolling
3 heaped tsp baking powder
50g caster sugar
175g salted butter, cubed
3 medium eggs
425ml whole milk
40g granulated sugar
jam and cream, to serve**
For the egg wash
**1 medium egg
1 dessertspoon milk**

1 Preheat the oven to 240°C, fan 220°C, gas 9. Sieve the plain flour and baking powder together into a large, wide bowl, then add a pinch of salt and the caster sugar. Thoroughly combine these dry ingredients with your hands, lifting them up to incorporate as much air as you can.

2 Toss the cubed butter well in the flour, then use the tips of your fingers to rub in the butter until the mixture resembles large flakes.

3 Whisk the eggs and the milk together in a separate bowl, then make a well in the centre of the flour mixture and pour all the liquid into it. With the fingers of one hand outstretched, mix the liquid in using full, circular movements from the centre to the outside of the bowl until it forms a dough.

4 Turn the dough out on to a work surface dusted with flour. Wash and dry your hands at this point, then tidy the dough around the edges, flip it over and roll or pat it gently into a round about 2.5cm thick. Use a 7.5cm plain cutter to cut out the scones. Periodically dip your cutter in some flour to stop it from sticking to the dough and stamp out the scones.

5 Gently gather the extra pieces of dough together, flatten them to the same thickness again and repeat until you have used all the dough.

6 Mix the egg and milk for the egg wash, brush the scones with it, then dip the tops in the granulated sugar.

7 Place the scones on a baking sheet and bake on the centre shelf of the preheated oven for 12-15 minutes, until golden brown. Transfer to a wire rack and allow to cool.

8 Serve the scones freshly baked, split in half with jam and cream.

■ 299cals; 11.2g fat (6.3g sat fat); 7.2g protein; 2.1g fibre; 42.3g carbs; 6.8g total sugars; 0.29g salt

ALSO TRY
Lemon scones
Add the grated zest of 1 **lemon** to the dry ingredients for the scones.

Candied citrus-peel scones
Add 100g finely chopped **candied orange and lemon peel** to the dry ingredients after rubbing in the butter.

Sultana scones
Add 100g **plump sultanas** to the dry ingredients after the butter has been rubbed in.

Poppy seed scones
Add 4 tablespoons **poppy seeds** to the dry ingredients after the butter has been rubbed in.

Chocolate-chip scones
Finely chop 100g deluxe **Belgian dark chocolate** and add to the dry ingredients after the butter has been rubbed in.

Cinnamon scones
Add 4 teaspoons **ground cinnamon** to the dry ingredients. Mix 1 teaspoon of **ground cinnamon** with 40g **granulated sugar** for the topping.

Craisin scones
Add 100g of **dried cranberries** to the dry ingredients after the butter has been rubbed in.

Lorraine Pascale

Lorraine's brownies are easy, decadent and very chocolatey – a great twist on a classic and so simple to whip up for teatime

Lorraine Pascale left the catwalk to follow her love for baking, has sold over a million cookery books and presented three television series. Lorraine also owns The Cupcake Bakehouse and has another television series and more books in the pipeline. We will be first in the queue to buy them!

Cookies and cream fudge brownies

Makes 16
Prep 15 mins **Total time** 45 mins, plus cooling
Get ahead The brownies will keep for a day or two. They freeze well, too

175g butter, plus extra
for greasing
200g dark chocolate,
finely chopped
3 large eggs and 2 large egg yolks
seeds of 1 vanilla pod, or 2 drops
of vanilla extract
175g light brown soft sugar
2 tbsp plain flour
1 tbsp cocoa powder
1 x 154g pack Oreo cookies,
broken into pieces
icing sugar, for dusting

1 Preheat the oven to 180°C, fan 160°C, gas 4. Grease a 20cm square baking tin and line with nonstick baking paper so that the paper slightly overlaps the sides of the tin.
2 Melt the butter in a pan, then remove from the heat and add the chocolate. Leave for a few minutes until the chocolate softens, then stir together.
3 Whisk the eggs, egg yolks and vanilla in a bowl until light and fluffy. Add the sugar in two lots, pouring it in around the edge of the mixture so you don't knock out the air, and whisk until the mixture becomes stiffer. Pour in the chocolate mixture around the edge and mix gently.
4 Add the flour, cocoa powder, a pinch of salt and a third of the Oreos. Stir, then pour into the tin. Press the remaining Oreos onto the mixture. Bake on the middle shelf of the oven for 25-30 minutes – it should be slightly gooey in the middle.
5 Leave to cool in the tin, then lift out using the baking paper and cut into squares. Dust with icing sugar.
■ 272cals; 17g fat (10g sat fat); 4g protein; 1g fibre; 27g carbs; 22g total sugars; 0.4g salt

Marble pistachio cake

With its pale green icing topped with chopped pistachios, this easy marble cake looks so pretty and tempting. Recipe by *Annie Bell*

Serves 12

Prep 45 mins **Total time** 1 hr 30 mins, plus cooling and setting

Get ahead It will keep for a few days in an airtight container. Can be frozen (uniced)

- 175g soft unsalted butter
- 225g caster sugar
- 3 medium eggs
- 100ml milk
- 225g self-raising flour, sifted
- 1½ tsp baking powder, sifted
- 50g shelled pistachios
- 50g ground almonds
- 1 tsp almond essence or extract
- green food colouring (liquid or paste)

For the icing

- 100g icing sugar, sifted
- ½ tsp almond essence or extract
- green food colouring (liquid or paste)
- 1 tbsp finely chopped pistachios

1 Preheat the oven to 190°C, fan 170°C, gas 5. Cream the butter and sugar together in a food processor, or in a bowl with an electric hand whisk, until pale and creamy. Beat in the eggs one at a time then mix in the milk. Don't worry if the mixture appears curdled at this point. Add the flour and baking powder and whisk until creamy, then divide the mixture between two bowls.

2 Whiz the pistachios in a food processor until finely ground. Fold the almonds into one half of the cake mixture and the pistachios, almond essence and a little green food colouring into the other half. Drop alternate spoonfuls of each mixture into a buttered and floured 22cm bundt (or ring) mould. Gently smooth the surface.

3 Bake for 30-35 minutes until golden and risen, and a skewer inserted into the cake comes out clean. Run a knife around the edges of the cake and leave to cool in the tin for 10 minutes. Then turn on to a cooling rack and leave to cool completely.

4 Blend the icing sugar with 1 tablespoon of water, the almond essence and a little colouring. Add a couple more drops of water at a time until you achieve a thick consistency. Drizzle over the cake, then scatter the chopped pistachios over the top. Leave to set for at least an hour.

■ 332cals; 17g fat (11g sat fat); 6g protein; 0.8g fibre; 43g carbs; 30g total sugars; 0.4g salt

KITCHEN *Secret*

If you don't have a bundt tin, this cake works just as well in a 23cm springform tin.

Pear and blueberry muffins

Children will love **Sarah Randell**'s spicy, fruity little muffins, which are perfect for lunchboxes or after-school teas

Makes 12
Prep 25 mins
Total time 1 hr, plus cooling
Get ahead Make a few hours ahead; best eaten on the same day

150g butter
1 ripe pear
1 medium carrot
150ml milk
175g caster sugar
3 medium eggs
300g self-raising flour
1 rounded tsp baking powder
3 tsp mixed spice
125g blueberries
For the lemon icing
75g icing sugar
about 3 tsp lemon juice

1 Preheat the oven to 200°C, fan 180°C, gas 6 and line a 12-hole muffin tin with paper cases. Melt the butter and leave to cool slightly. Core and chop the pear into small pieces; trim and grate the carrot – no need to peel either.

2 In a large mixing bowl, whisk together the milk, sugar, eggs and melted butter to combine.

3 Add the flour, baking powder, mixed spice, blueberries, pear and grated carrot. Using a large spoon, fold everything together. Divide the mixture between the muffin cases. Bake for 30 minutes or until well risen. Leave to cool.

4 For the icing, mix the icing sugar with enough lemon juice to make a drizzling consistency – add the juice little by little. Drizzle the muffins with icing and leave to set.

■ 302cals; 13g fat (7g sat fat); 5g protein; 2g fibre; 44g carbs; 5g total sugars; 0.6g salt

ALSO TRY
Blackberry and apple muffins
Use an eating **apple** instead of the pear, and **blackberries** – an autumn favourite – instead of the blueberries.

KITCHEN *Secret*

Short of time? Dust with icing sugar instead of making icing, and eat warm.

Chocolate meringue kisses

Delicate mini meringues to bake and gift, *Lorraine Pascale* showed us this recipe on a magazine shoot with her in 2011 and we were hooked!

Makes 25

Prep 35 mins **Total time** 1 hr 45 mins

Get ahead Unsandwiched meringues will keep in an airtight box for up to a week and can be frozen. Make the buttercream the day before, chill; bring to room temperature to sandwich the meringues up to 2 hours before serving

175g pecans
5 large egg whites
a squeeze of lemon juice
¼ tsp cream of tartar
275g caster sugar
For the chocolate buttercream
150g soft butter
300g icing sugar, sifted
5 tbsp chocolate hazelnut spread
2 tbsp milk

1 Preheat the oven to 200°C, fan 180°C, gas 6. Spread the pecans on a baking tray; toast in the oven for 8 minutes. When cool, whiz in a food processor until finely ground. Lower the oven to 120°C, fan 100°C, gas ½.

2 Line three baking trays with nonstick baking paper. Using an electric mixer or hand whisk, whisk the egg whites and lemon juice to stiff peaks. Whisking all the time, add the cream of tartar and the sugar, a few tablespoons at a time. Keep on whisking until you have a stiff, shiny meringue. Stir in the ground pecans.

3 In batches, spoon the meringue mixture into a piping bag with a star nozzle and pipe 50 x 3-4cm blobs on to the baking trays. Bake for 1 hour; leave to cool on the trays.

4 For the buttercream, cream the butter with an electric mixer or hand whisk until light and fluffy. Add the icing sugar, whisking well, and mix in the chocolate spread and milk. Sandwich the meringues together with the chocolate buttercream.

■ 203cals; 11g fat (4g sat fat); 1.4g protein; 0.4g fibre; 26g carbs; 25g total sugars; 0.1g salt

KITCHEN *Secret*

No piping bag? Spoon the meringue into a disposable food bag and snip off a corner to pipe even meringues.

Toffee fudge chunk cookies

A failsafe cookie recipe – try inventing your own nut and fruit variations, and watch them disappear from the cookie jar

Makes 12
Prep 15 mins **Total time** 45 mins, plus cooling
Get ahead Make a few days in advance; store in an airtight box. Can be frozen raw (see tip below) or baked

- 125g soft unsalted butter
- 125g dark brown soft sugar
- 2 tbsp condensed milk
- 175g self-raising flour, sifted
- 100g fudge chunks
- 200g dark chocolate, melted

1 Preheat the oven to 150°C, fan 130°C, gas 2. Using an electric hand whisk or mixer, cream the butter and sugar together until pale and fluffy.

2 Beat in the condensed milk, then add the flour and a pinch of salt and mix. Stir in half the fudge chunks.

3 Roll into 12 walnut-sized balls and space at least 5cm apart on 2 baking sheets lined with baking paper, then flatten them slightly with the back of a spoon. Sprinkle the remaining fudge chunks over the cookies.

4 Bake for about 25 minutes, until firm at the edges but still soft in the middle. Leave to cool for a few minutes before transferring to a cooling rack.

5 Dip half of each cooled cookie in the melted chocolate, allow to set.

■ 293cals; 14.9g fat (9.3g sat fat); 2.7g protein; 1.2g fibre; 37.4g carbs; 27.9g total sugars; 0.18g salt

ALSO TRY
Maple syrup pecan cookies
Step 2: Use 2 tablespoons **maple syrup** instead of the condensed milk. Chop 100g **pecan halves** to replace the fudge, keeping 12 halves aside for decoration.
Step 3: Top each cookie with a reserved pecan half before baking. Leave to cool.
Step 5: Omit the melted chocolate.

Cherry and almond cookies
Step 2: Replace the fudge chunks with 75g chopped **glacé cherries**.
Step 3: Sprinkle each cookie with a few **flaked almonds** before baking.
Step 5: Omit the melted chocolate.

KITCHEN *Secret*

The cookies can be baked from frozen – just add an extra 5 minutes to the cooking time.

Eric Lanlard

Light-as-air sponge with a colourful fruit filling – Eric's showstopper cake is a summertime favourite

Eric is a Master Pâtissier and has created impressive cakes for a host of A-listers. Having worked for Albert and Michel Roux, Eric now has his own cake business, Cake Boy in South London. We always enjoy watching him on his *Baking Mad* television series and Eric is a regular contributor to *Sainsbury's magazine*. He has written several books including *Home Bake*, *Tart it Up!* and *Chocolat*.

Summer berry cake

Serves 16
Prep 35 mins **Total time** 1 hr,
plus cooling

> 250g golden caster sugar
> 8 large eggs
> 250g plain flour
> 50g unsalted butter, melted
> *For the filling*
> 400ml double cream
> 2 tsp vanilla (or caster) sugar
> 750g mixed berries
> small mint leaves and icing sugar,
> to finish

1 Preheat the oven to 180°C, fan 160°C,
gas 4. Put the sugar and eggs in a
heatproof bowl and set it over a pan of
simmering water – don't let the bottom
of the bowl touch the water. Whisk,
using an electric hand whisk, for
15 minutes until the mixture thickens
and doubles in volume. Remove the
bowl from the pan of hot water.

2 In batches, sift the flour onto the
mixture and gently fold in with a
large metal spoon. Now fold in the
melted butter, but don't overmix.
Divide the mixture between two
20cm x 4cm-deep sandwich tins that
have been greased and dusted with
flour. Smooth the tops and bake for
25 minutes until golden. Turn out
onto a wire rack to cool completely.

3 Slice the sponges in half horizontally
with a serrated knife to make 4 layers.
Whip the cream with the vanilla sugar.

4 To assemble, put the bottom layer on a
cake stand and spread with the whipped
cream. Layer some berries on top, slicing
the strawberries, cover with another
layer of cream and put the second
sponge on top. Top this sponge with
cream only, then add the third sponge.
Cover with cream, berries and cream as
before, then place the final sponge on
top. Cover with the remaining cream and
berries. Decorate with the mint leaves
and dust with icing sugar.

■ 329cals; 20g fat (11g sat fat);
7g protein; 2g fibre; 30g carbs;
19g total sugars; 0.1g salt

Passionfruit drizzle traybake

This easy-to-make traybake by *Annie Bell* takes lemon drizzle cake to a whole new level with the addition of fragrant, zingy passionfruit

Serves 12
Prep 20 mins **Total time** 50 mins, plus cooling
Get ahead Make up a day ahead; it freezes well, too

- 225g soft unsalted butter
- 225g golden caster sugar
- 3 medium eggs
- 150ml milk
- 225g self-raising flour, sifted
- 1 tsp baking powder, sifted
- finely grated zest of 1 orange
- juice of ½ orange and ½ lemon
- pulp of 3 passionfruit
- 100g golden granulated sugar

1 Preheat the oven to 190°C, fan 170°C, gas 5. Butter a 30 x 23cm x 4cm-deep baking tin. Put the butter and caster sugar in the bowl of a food processor and mix together until pale and fluffy, or use a large bowl and an electric hand whisk. Whisk in the eggs one at a time, scraping down the sides of the bowl if necessary, then add the milk.

Don't worry if the mixture appears curdled at this point. Gradually add the flour and baking powder through the funnel with the motor running, finally adding the orange zest.

2 Transfer the mixture to the baking tin, smoothing the surface, and bake for 30 minutes or until golden and shrinking slightly from the sides, and a skewer comes out clean from the centre.

3 Run a knife around the edge of the tin and prick the cake with a skewer all over the surface at about 2cm intervals. Combine the orange and lemon juices, passionfruit pulp and granulated sugar in a bowl, stirring until evenly mixed, then spoon this over the top of the warm cake. Leave it to cool, allowing the juice to sink into the cake. Once cool, cut into squares.

■ 360cals; 19g fat (9g sat fat); 4.2g protein; 1g fibre; 44g carbs; 29g total sugars; 0.3g salt

KITCHEN *Secret*

This bake is also delicious served warm as a pudding – serve with crème fraîche.

Crystallised flower cupcakes

As pretty as a picture, *Fiona Cairns*' individual cupcakes decorated with flowers look just as dramatic as one big cake for a celebration

Makes 18

Prep 30 mins **Total time** 40 mins, plus setting time

Get ahead Make and ice the cakes up to 3 days in advance and store in plastic containers in a cool place, or they can be frozen before icing

75g self-raising flour, sifted
25g cocoa powder, sifted
½ tsp baking powder
100g very soft unsalted butter
100g light muscovado sugar
2 large eggs, lightly beaten
1 tbsp milk

To decorate
300g icing sugar
pink and/or green food colouring, (liquid or paste)
edible crystallised flowers or petals (see tip, opposite)

1 Preheat the oven to 180°C, fan 160°C, gas 4. Place all the ingredients, except the milk, in a food processor and whiz until just mixed together. Add the milk and briefly whiz again. Alternatively, beat together by hand.

2 Line 18 holes of 2 x 12-hole bun trays with paper or foil cupcake cases. If you don't have 2 bun trays, just cook the cakes in batches.

3 Put 2 rounded teaspoons of the mixture in each case and bake for 10-12 minutes, or until springy to the touch. It will seem like a scant amount of mixture in each case but you need room for the icing. Repeat with the rest of the mixture until it is used up.

4 To decorate, sift the icing sugar into a bowl and slowly stir in 2-3 tablespoons of water. The icing should be the consistency of custard. Add a mere touch of the food colouring to the bowl, then mix. You're aiming for a pale pastel colour; add a touch more colour if needed. Pour about a dessertspoon of icing onto each cake. Leave for a few hours to set before decorating with edible crystallised flowers or petals.

■ 157cals; 5.8g fat (3.4g sat fat); 1.7g protein; 0.4g fibre; 24.7g carbs; 21.9g total sugars; 0.14g salt

ALSO TRY
Lemon cupcakes

Use 100g **self-raising flour**; omit the cocoa powder. Replace the muscovado sugar with **caster sugar**. Use the finely grated zest of half a **lemon** and 1 tablespoon **lemon juice** in place of the milk. For the icing, use 2-3 tablespoons **lemon juice** instead of the water.

ALSO TRY
Cream cheese frosting

Melt 75g **unsalted butter** in a small pan and leave to cool slightly. Whisk together 75g **caster sugar** and 150g chilled **cream cheese**. Add the melted butter and a drop or two of **food colouring** if you want to colour the frosting, and whisk again. Chill the frosting before piping or spreading onto the cakes. Finish with **sprinkles**. Makes enough for 18 cupcakes.

'A PIECE OF THIS FOR AFTERNOON TEA
IS LIKE A *little slice of heaven*'

Triple chocolate cake

A failsafe chocolate cake for all occasions – dust with icing sugar for a teatime treat or doll it up with chocolate curls for a birthday

Serves 12
Prep 30 mins **Total time** 1 hr, plus cooling and setting
Get ahead The sponges can be baked up to a day ahead; store in airtight containers. They freeze well too. The cake can be assembled a few hours ahead; keep chilled

> 100g soft butter
> 275g caster sugar
> ½ tsp vanilla extract
> 250g self-raising flour
> 50g cocoa powder
> 1 tsp bicarbonate of soda
> 3 large eggs, separated
> *For the filling and icing*
> 2 x 200g bars milk chocolate
> 4 tbsp milk chocolate spread
> 50g dark chocolate
> 50g white chocolate

1 Preheat the oven to 180°C, fan 160°C, gas 4. Lightly butter two 20cm x 4cm-deep loose-bottomed sponge tins and line them with nonstick baking paper. In a bowl, using an electric hand whisk, cream the butter, 200g of the sugar and the vanilla extract together until pale and fluffy.

2 In another bowl, sift together the flour, cocoa powder, bicarbonate of soda and a pinch of salt, then beat into the butter and sugar mixture a little at a time alternately with the egg yolks and 250ml cold water.

3 In a large clean bowl, whisk the egg whites to soft peaks then whisk in the remaining sugar, a tablespoon at a time, until stiff and shiny. Fold the egg white into the chocolate mixture, then divide between two prepared tins and bake for 25-30 minutes, until a skewer comes out clean.

4 Cool the cakes in the tins for 5 minutes, then turn out on to a wire rack, peel off the baking paper and leave to cool completely.

5 In a bowl, melt 300g of the milk chocolate over a pan of simmering water, stirring occasionally, making sure the bowl doesn't touch the water. Remove from the pan and leave to cool slightly.

6 Sandwich the cakes together with the chocolate spread. Spoon some of the melted milk chocolate over the cake then, using a palette knife, smooth it over the top and sides of the cake, adding more chocolate until it is coated. Cool and then leave to set in the fridge for 30 minutes.

7 Using a vegetable peeler, shave curls off the remaining milk chocolate and the dark and white chocolate (it helps if the chocolate is at warm room temperature to do this) and sprinkle the curls over the cake.

■ 519cals; 25.2g fat, (13.8g sat fat); 69.4g carbs; 8.2g protein; 1.6g fibre; 49g total sugars; 0.8g salt

KITCHEN *Secret*

For a children's birthday cake, cover the cake in multi-coloured Smarties instead of the curls.

Sticky fig and almond cakes

Figs look so pretty on cakes and go really well with almonds. Serve these with Greek yogurt. Recipe by *Sarah Randell*

Makes 6
Prep 15 mins **Total time** 35 mins
Get ahead Make up to the end of step 3 a few hours ahead. Can be frozen, too

- **125g butter**
- **100g plain flour**
- **125g icing sugar**
- **75g ground almonds**
- **zest of 1 lemon**
- **4 large egg whites**
- **6 figs, thinly sliced**
For the syrup
- **100g golden syrup**
- **1 vanilla pod, halved lengthways and seeds removed**
- **a squeeze of lemon juice**

1 Preheat the oven to 200°C, fan 180°C, gas 6. Melt the butter and set aside to cool slightly. Sift the flour and icing sugar into a large bowl. Stir in the ground almonds and lemon zest.
2 Whisk the egg whites to soft peaks and fold them into the dry mixture, a little at a time, alternating with the cooled melted butter.
3 Generously butter a six-hole muffin tin and line the bases with circles of nonstick baking paper. Divide the cake mixture between the holes of the tin. Top each cake with a few slices of fig. Bake in the preheated oven for 20-25 minutes or until risen and lightly golden. Line a baking tray with nonstick baking paper and bake the remaining fig slices for a few minutes towards the end of the cooking time.
4 To make the syrup, gently heat the golden syrup with the vanilla seeds and lemon juice.
5 Drizzle each cake with syrup, then top with a few of the extra baked fig slices and generously drizzle again. Eat warm or cold.

■ 451cals; 25g fat (12g sat fat); 7g protein; 1.7g fibre; 54g carbs; 41g total sugars; 0.5g salt

KITCHEN
Secret

These are also delicious served with ice cream. Try them topped with sliced strawberries instead of figs, too.

Menu ideas

Whether it's an easy midweek meal, a drinks party with seriously scrumptious nibbles or a stylish dinner to impress your friends, take inspiration from our recipes and try these menu suggestions

A simple midweek supper

Flamme tart, **p46**
Mascarpone, rum and lime creams, **p143**

Cosy afternoon tea

Lemon scones, **p166**
Toffee fudge chunk cookies, **p177**
Triple chocolate cake, **p185**

A celebration drinks party

Florentine pizzettes, **p31**
Coconut prawn fritters, **p31**
Chilli coriander sausage rolls, **p31**
Clementine Prosecco cocktail, **p31**
Beef sliders with red onion pickle, **p118**

A buffet for a crowd

Chicken, pancetta and prune terrine, **p24**
Thai-style gravadlax with coriander and lime dressing, **p29**
Aubergine with buttermilk sauce, **p49**
Pissaladière, **p99**
Peperonata, **p127**
Zingy slaw, **p118**
Pavlova with nectarines, redcurrants, and elderflower syllabub, **p145**
Chocolate orange cheesecake, **p146**

A vegetarian feast

Crispy tofu salad with ginger, **p45**
Sri Lankan cashew nut curry, **p105**
White chocolate mousse brûlées with prunes, **p149**

Saturday night at home with friends

Roquefort cheese soufflés, **p21**
Basil leaf and Parma ham-wrapped prawns with lemon and basil risotto, **p91**
Buttermilk panna cottas with roasted plums, **p151**

Sunday lunch

Parsley soup with caper and tomato salsa, **p16**
Italian stuffed roast pork, **p92**
Sweet potato and celeriac mash, **p135**
Ribboned carrots with honey and parsley, **p137**
Pear, ginger and chocolate cobbler, **p162**

Weights		Volume		Measurements		Oven temperatures		
							fan	gas
15g	½oz	25ml	1fl oz	2mm	1/16 in	110°C	90°C	
25g	1oz	50ml	2fl oz	3mm	⅛ in	120°C	100°C	½
40g	1½oz	75ml	3fl oz	4mm	⅙ in	140°C	120°C	1
50g	2oz	100ml	4fl oz	5mm	¼ in	150°C	130°C	2
60g	2½oz	150ml	5fl oz (¼ pint)	1cm	½ in	160°C	140°C	3
75g	3oz	175ml	6fl oz	2cm	¾ in	180°C	160°C	4
100g	3½oz	200ml	7fl oz	2.5cm	1in	190°C	170°C	5
125g	4oz	225ml	8fl oz	3cm	1¼ in	200°C	180°C	6
150g	5oz	250ml	9fl oz	4cm	1½ in	220°C	200°C	7
175g	6oz	300ml	10fl oz (½ pint)	4.5cm	1¾ in	230°C	210°C	8
200g	7oz	350ml	13fl oz	5cm	2in	240°C	220°C	9
225g	8oz	400ml	14fl oz	6cm	2½ in			
250g	9oz	450ml	16fl oz (¾ pint)	7.5cm	3in			
275g	10oz	600ml	20fl oz (1 pint)	9cm	3½ in			
300g	11oz	750ml	25fl oz (1¼ pints)	10cm	4in			
350g	12oz	900ml	30fl oz (1½ pints)	13cm	5in			
375g	13oz	1 litre	34fl oz (1¾ pints)	13.5cm	5¼ in			
400g	14oz	1.2 litres	40fl oz (2 pints)	15cm	6in			
425g	15oz	1.5 litres	52fl oz (2½ pints)	16cm	6½ in			
450g	1lb	1.8 litres	60fl oz (3 pints)	18cm	7in			
500g	1lb 2oz			19cm	7½ in			
650g	1lb 7oz			20cm	8in			
675g	1½lb			23cm	9in			
700g	1lb 9oz			24cm	9½ in			
750g	1lb 11oz			25.5cm	10 in			
900g	2lb			28cm	11 in			
1kg	2lb 4oz			30cm	12 in			
1.5kg	3lb 6oz			32.5cm	13 in			
				35cm	14 in			

Unless otherwise stated, tin, pan and dish measurements in recipes are of the base, and spoon measures are level.

Food
Food director Sarah Randell
Cookery assistant Emma Franklin
Recipe testing Jenna Leiter, Vicky Pettipher

Additional recipes
Emma Franklin, Ghillie James, Lucy Jessop, Sarah Randell, Kate Titford

Design
Senior art director Liz Baird
Art director David Jenkins
Picture Editor Leanne Bracey

Editorial
Editor Helena Lang
Production editor Ward Hellewell

Photography
Food Martin Poole (8, 11, 13, 29, 32, 38, 44, 47, 49, 50, 56, 58, 65, 76, 79, 86, 90, 97, 98, 101, 106, 111, 112, 116, 127, 128,, 140, 143, 151, 153, 159, 163, 164, 167, 176, 179), Dan Jones (43, 60, 63, 64, 72, 73, 78, 81, 82, 83, 102, 105, 118, 121, 130, 134, 69), Jonathan Gregson (14, 18, 52, 70, 84, 125, 138, 160, 161), Tara Fisher (17, 68, 95, 115, 131, 133), Laura Edwards (41, 137, 144, 157, 187), Philip Webb (22, 30, 35, 55, 85), Peter Cassidy (51, 148, 182, 183), Anders Schønnemann (27, 146, 147, 154), Con Poulos (171, 175, 180), Jan Baldwin (139, 172), Vanessa Courtier (75), Georgia Glynn Smith (122), Richard Jung (37), Jonathan Kennedy (21), Gareth Morgans (80), Michael Paul (25), Charlie Richards (67), Brett Stevens (109), Yuki Sugiura (184), Karen Thomas (89, 93), Kate Whitaker (119)

Portraits Tara Fisher (62, 94, 136), Jan Baldwin (4), Simon Brown (36), Hugo Burnand (142), Vanessa Courtier (74), Chris Everard (26), Jonathan Gregson (20), Rama Knight (178), Emma Lee (150), Myles New (168), Keiko Oikawa (48), Sam Pelly (126), Brett Stevens (104).

Additional pictures Christian Barnett, Hugo Burnand, Vanessa Courtier, Chris Everard, Rama Knight, David Loftus, Martin Poole.

For Sainsbury's
Phil Carroll
Sharon Nightingale
Mavis Sarfo

Print & Production
Production manager Mike Lamb
Colour origination Altaimage Ltd
Printed by Butler Tanner & Dennis Ltd, Frome and London

Thanks to...
Patricia Baker, Lynne de Lacy, Clare Devane, Fiona Hunter, Katrina Rendall

seven.co.uk

© Produced by Seven Publishing on behalf of Sainsbury's Supermarkets Ltd, 33 Holborn, London EC1N 2HT.

Notes

*Pick up this month's
Sainsbury's magazine